CW01095378

I Love My Life

A healing heart journey from
trauma to triumph..

CHARLOTTE LEWIS

BALBOA.PRESS

A DIVISION OF HAY HOUSE

Balboa Press books may be ordered through booksellers or by contacting:

Balboa Press
A Division of Hay House
1663 Liberty Drive
Bloomington, IN 47403
www.balboapress.com
844-682-1282

Because of the dynamic nature of the Internet, any web addresses or
links contained in this book may have changed since publication and
may no longer be valid. The views expressed in this work are solely those
of the author and do not necessarily reflect the views of the publisher,
and the publisher hereby disclaims any responsibility for them.

The author of this book does not dispense medical advice or prescribe the use
of any technique as a form of treatment for physical, emotional, or medical
problems without the advice of a physician, either directly or indirectly. The
intent of the author is only to offer information of a general nature to help
you in your quest for emotional and spiritual well-being. In the event you use
any of the information in this book for yourself, which is your constitutional
right, the author and the publisher assume no responsibility for your actions.

Any people depicted in stock imagery provided by Getty Images are
models, and such images are being used for illustrative purposes only.
Certain stock imagery © Getty Images.

Cover image by Clarence Kingsley-Pillai

Print information available on the last page.

ISBN: 979-8-7652-4299-5 (sc)
ISBN: 979-8-7652-4301-5 (hc)
ISBN: 979-8-7652-4300-8 (e)

Library of Congress Control Number: 2023910970

Balboa Press rev. date: 07/05/2023

Dedication: I dedicate this story to Bob, who said to me before he died, "I think we have pretty much cleared our karma with one another in this lifetime together, Char."

And so, for Bob, in honor of the deep love and the destiny we once shared. May our families understand that this is solely 'my' truth and grant me forgiveness for any sorrow wrought by my words.

Contents

Chapter 1

A Decision to Heal

Sitting outside on my front porch sipping my morning coffee, gazing at the green rolling hills in the distance, I inhaled the strong sweet smell of lilacs that pierced the air as they burst into bloom after last night's rain. I was feeling a deep abiding sense of contentment when my phone rang, and I wondered who might be calling me on this early Sunday morning in May. The voice of a dear old friend lifted my spirits even more than the lilacs, for we share a history of having been friends since our youth. Seniors now, our friendship measures fifty years and counting. All of our talks are like a soft landing pad, a safe place of understanding, mutual admiration and respect that hardly needs words anymore. So, my quiet moment of contentment amplifies into joy as I anticipate sharing whatever might come up in conversation.

"How are you?" She casually asked.

I think I took her by surprise with my answer even as I surprised myself – as we so often do in conversation when sentiments come to the surface unexpectedly. I felt a kind of whole-body effervescence when I replied that I honestly felt happier than I ever had in my life.

"I love my life," I exclaimed with deepest sincerity.

However unexpected, as soon as I said this, I realized it was true. I had come through. It was amazing because it didn't seem that long ago that I was at the end of my rope and didn't know whether I would live or die.

My friend understood how amazing it was for me to be feeling this way, because she had watched me struggle through the last few years of my life not knowing whether I could survive the drama and the trauma of all that life had brought my way. Six short years before I had been in the throes of, *It can't get any worse than this,* And, *I just can't take it anymore.* I knew I needed to find a way to heal my life. There was a moment in time I absolutely knew this to be true. That if I didn't find my way back to some nebulous place of belonging that I had abandoned within myself, I would give up on life and welcome death. I had no idea what that search really meant, what it would look like, or all that the healing journey would entail, but I knew I had to try.

The healing journey that I was about to take would be about finding my way home to myself; to a place where I could feel safe again, where I could feel worthy and loved. I had lost all of that and more somewhere along the way, and the self-imposed exile that once kept me safe and protected now felt lonely and no longer safe. I felt defeated, fragile, and vulnerable — really and truly broken. This healing journey I was about to embark on would be one of personal growth and transformation.

I began to question what kind of things precipitate the shift that finds us on the threshold of major change and set us on the path of a healing journey. Is it fear, confusion, crisis, conflict, illness, loss, divorce, or the death of a loved one? Is it broken dreams, or a broken heart? Whether one or more (or all of the above as I felt it was for me), there comes a time when the journey becomes undeniably crucial, because the alternative is nothing short of final. When the alternative is death, you may suddenly recognize that you've been dying a slow death for some time already. This happens in small ways that go unnoticed even to yourself, but the changes suddenly become blatantly apparent until they are impossible to ignore.

It is during this intimate recognition of unrelenting pain, of heartbreak and despair, that we begin to open to the possibility of true healing. *The wound itself becomes the fertile ground for healing and for growth.* Rumi said it well.

"Keep your gaze on the wounded place; that is where the light enters."

And so it was for me as I stared cancer in its face, as I admitted defeat in a forty-year marriage (saying goodbye to a lost love), and then another farewell as I kept vigil at the bedside of my dying sister. I was one big hot mess. Suffering that acute brings you to your knees and kicks you in the ass. It's an enormous challenge when you find yourself standing on the threshold of knowing you can't compromise yourself anymore but not knowing where the hell to start making changes.

So, my journey began — the journey home to myself that only I could navigate. This was my journey until the path became clearer and clearer; until I could finally see the light at the end of the tunnel. It wasn't that brilliant light that we are told we experience in transition to death. It was the light of life. Now I knew that it wouldn't be outside of myself that I would find the answers to heal my body, my troubled mind, and my broken heart. The answers could only be found *within*. It's an inside job.

The first thing I would discover was that healing your heart, your body, and ultimately your *life*, takes hard work... and we're not likely to find the motivation or the commitment to do the hard work unless we're in such a deep, dark place of despair that there isn't a choice anymore. If trauma or crisis in itself is the essential prerequisite to taking that first tentative step on a profound healing journey, then motivation and commitment must follow. I would even venture to guess that the deeper the trauma or the bigger the crisis, the more likelihood there is that a person will be adamant that they're ready for change — and ready to do the work. This work, if fully embraced, will inevitably lead to that glorious outcome of, "I love my life!"

I had been working as a private practice counselor and family therapist for just over ten years when I found myself in dire need of finding a counselor for myself. I called my private practice "Healing Heart Counseling" because I believe that it is in our hearts that we carry our pain. We may carry discomfort and disease in our bodies, confusion and mental anguish in our minds, but when emotions take hold, we feel them in our heart of hearts. I believe almost everyone in the world knows what a broken heart feels like because everyone has experienced loss of one kind or another. Examples are, the loss of loyalty when a friend turns away or hurts your feelings, the loss of trust when someone deceives you, the loss of faith when you can't fathom the meaning in all of the suffering in the world.

I also believe that the world is in transition toward more of a heart-based society because so many in the world today are seeking resolution from unrelenting discontent in their lives. I sense there is a new movement toward a more benevolent planet of people. These people are choosing to live differently, from the inside-out rather than from being dictated by society, or living in reaction to whatever is happening out in the world and out of their control. People are thinking twice before taking the word of politicians and other people of power and are seeking to find the answers that feel true for them and are ultimately moving inward toward self-empowerment. A conscious choice to heal in a self-directed way can't help but be a catalyst for empowerment, even as we take that first tentative step — battered and broken but with intention.

In the late 1980's when my mother was diagnosed with breast cancer, I was introduced to Louise Hay's work and began to understand mind/body connections and the notion that our mental and emotional states manifest as pain, disease and symptoms of diagnosis in our bodies. A pioneer in the field of holistic health, Hays' book, *You can Heal Your Life*, became the quintessential handbook for proactive individuals striving to empower themselves in healing. I would use Louise's concepts in my cognitive behavioral approach in counseling others, and most certainly incorporated them into my personal growth work, but it wouldn't be until 25 years later that I would need to take my understanding on this subject to a whole new level and would forge my way through a very intense healing journey of my own. Hays' little blue pocketbook, *You Can Heal Your Body*, had been a constant companion for me throughout the years. Even so, like so many others, I only consulted it when a physiological challenge presented itself. I would scan the index to find the appropriate area of the body where I was experiencing symptoms, and faithfully repeat aloud over and over again, the appropriate positive affirmation that is meant to combat the problem, and this worked for me.

Some thirty years later I would re-read, *You Can Heal Your Life*, and I would augment that with many of the more recent self-help books that fly off the shelves two decades into the new millennium. Michael Singers' *The Untethered Soul*; Anita Moorjani's *Dying To Be Me*; *Belonging* by Toko Pa Turner; and Caroline Myss's *Anatomy Of The Spirit* are but a few of my favorites.

I would be absolutely blown away by Dr. Gabor Maté's publication, *When the Body Says No.* How accurately I could relate to everything he was saying about the personalities and the life circumstances of those that are diagnosed with cancer and autoimmune diseases. Maté gave further evidence and clarity to body/mind connections, and he found and documented the common denominators and the psychological profiles of hundreds of patients diagnosed with cancer and autoimmune diseases. Not surprisingly I fit the profiles perfectly! It was no wonder that I had just been diagnosed with Stage 4 cancer, and upon completion of my chemotherapy and radiation treatments was then diagnosed with an autoimmune disease that found me completely debilitated with the chronic pain of Rheumatoid Arthritis. This newfound awareness was certainly instrumental in sparking my intellectual interest, but as validating as it was to have discovered the wherefore and the why, I still remained at a loss about what to do to help myself heal. How might I 'reverse' the circumstances that brought me here?

Chapter 2

Surrender and Trust

THIS FIRST STEP ON MY JOURNEY WOULD BE A RELATIVELY EASY one. Not one made without a degree of conscious and concentrated intention on my part, but easy in that it didn't require that I actually 'do' a lot. This first step was one of 'Surrender' and 'Trust.'

The trust was two-fold. I promised myself that I would trust my instincts every step of the way, and I promised that I would trust the universe (or God).

I would find myself having to employ this first step time and time again over the ensuing five years. When all the hard work found me feeling discouraged and defeated along the way, I surrendered, and I trusted.

I learned that the old adages of 'maybe you're trying too hard' or 'get the hell out of your own way' rang true for me time and again. I was often so desperate to be proactive, and to do everything in my power to make the right choices and find the answers, it wasn't easy for me to 'let go' and succumb to a place of 'allowing,' of willingness to detach from the problems and the challenges at hand. But the quietude and stillness that accompanies a state of surrender is integral to learning to trust, both yourself, and life in general. It is when we turn down the noise and calm our mind that we give our intentions the space to rise up, and our inner voice the space to be heard so we can tap into our inner guidance. So, although it wasn't easy, in those early months of coping with my cancer diagnosis, with surgery and post-surgery chemo and radiation treatments, I would find myself *in complete surrender; in trusting that the Universe had my back, and in trusting that the universal energy of (healing)love and (healing)light would see me through.*

Surrendering is by no means giving up. Surrender is not meek or passive or waving the white flag to become a victim. Surrender is to let go of control, or to let go of the notion that we were ever in control to begin with.

Survival is the construct by which we learn to attempt controlling our realities in the first place, but our reality and sense of identity are only ever defined by our conditioning and our egos. It is our ego's strategy to constantly over analyze and strive to find out why and how and strategize the route. But, we don't need the map because the universe has the map. If we can let go of our conditioned mind (the one that is limited to our past experience and defines us by our pasts) and open ourselves up to curiosity and possibility through surrender, then life can begin to unfold in ways we hadn't ever imagined.

The degree to which we are 'conditioned' is the degree to which we are not free but are imprisoned in our egos. Our conditioned minds are the block to the magic and the miracles that surrender brings. You don't even necessarily have to *find* the place where you are stuck or blocked. The blockages that are keeping you stuck may be released inadvertently when you strive to remain in that state of peaceful surrender. It is often on the heels of extreme pain, when we are falling to our knees in despair, that we learn to lean in to surrender and we discover the relief surrender brings.

One of the keys to receiving guidance through surrender comes with the willingness to not know the future. Being able to accept uncertainty is to be in the knowing that you've given it your all, and now it's time to detach from the outcome in order to be able to surrender and trust. When we surrender to the will of the universe (or to the will of God if you prefer), we are also surrendering to something deep within ourselves that wants to emerge. In your willingness to let go of your personal agenda and sit in a place of your being that has stopped chattering and expecting, that surrender in itself will bring you clarity.

When we surrender to what the universe is seeking to make happen for us, we actually transcend our human limitations and open ourselves to the infinite potentials of life. In surrendering, we make room for hidden truths to make themselves known, for clues to surface, for answers to be heard. Our intuition becomes more finely tuned. *Healing ceases to happen to you, but instead through you.* In surrendering, we are connecting with the creative life force of the divine, which is *'sacred.'* This divine power renders our pain and suffering sacred which then defines our healing journey as a sacred one. Surrender can become one of your most powerful healing practices.

My healing journey was like a spiritual awakening for me. It was like a union with spirit. If in our suffering we have felt abandoned by the divine, then we must return to the place of trusting that we will *return to wholeness* as surely as the universe find us wholly sacred and divine. My ensuing prayers over the next five years would embrace the grace of surrendering, and of knowing I was held in the arms of Spirit.

If the notion of letting go seems way too difficult a task for you after years of wanting to remain in control and wanting to influence your outcomes with a multitude of strategies, consider that we are actually hard-wired to let go. We do so every time we exhale. Just let go. Exhale.

Chapter 3

Diagnosis and Treatment

I DON'T THINK THERE'S ANY OTHER STATEMENT THAT ROCKS YOUR world as swiftly as the words, "You have cancer." Hearing those words sets you in motion so fast you don't know what hit you. Though it is not the death sentence it once was for the advances that have been made in medical research and treatments, once a cancer diagnosis is present, it forever remains a lurking shadow by your side. It will immediately find you seeking every means possible to be healed.

It was in the spring of 2016 that I was diagnosed with Stage 4 Endometrial Clear Cell Carcinoma. I heard words like malignant and aggressive, and I understood that it was a serious concern because it had spread beyond the wall of my uterus to my bowel. A team of oncologists deliberated what the best course of action would be — surgery first and then treatment, or vice versa. I decided very early on in the process that I would follow my instincts through it all. At that point my instincts told me that if I didn't speak up with my preference, they wouldn't ask it of me. So, I voiced my thoughts and was glad that I chose a fast-track surgery when afterward I was told, "We believe we got it all."

The next oncology course of action would be 18 months of chemotherapy and radiation as a preventative measure to the cancer's return. Here, I was hesitant, because I secretly believed that measures I had taken prior to surgery may well have influenced the outcome, and those measures were anything but ordinary. They were holistic in nature, and I took them with absolute 'blind trust'.

In the months leading up to my diagnosis, my days were filled doing one job. That particular year I had taken a contract as a primary caregiver for an elderly lady who had unexpectedly lost her husband. She had advanced skin cancer that had eaten away a good part of one side of her face, and she suffered from a long-standing mental illness. She not only needed a caregiver but also someone who could pack up her house and get her moved into a long-term care facility. It was a big job.

She was a lovely lady, and I cherished my time with her. My brief association with her would prove to have a significant impact on my life. We would remain friends till her dying day when I sat by her bedside holding her hand as she gently slipped away to heaven.

Unfortunately, she and her husband had been hoarders, and their small 800 square foot house was packed to the brim! Their passions were organic gardening and holistic health, and every wall in their kitchen and living room was lined with bookshelves filled with hundreds of books on these subjects and others. The walk-in pantry held boxes and boxes full of every holistic health supplement you can imagine, as well as a freezer full of their organically grown produce.

In the process of packing up the books, she insisted on going through every title to decide whether it would go to the second hand bookstore, for donation to the local thrift store, or be moved to her new place. She gave me free reign to keep whatever titles I chose. I kept very few. For example, among at least 20 or 30 books on cancer I kept only one, for no particular reason whatsoever other than that it looked interesting.

In the process of cleaning up the pantry I was advised to throw out all the expired vitamins and supplements. However, again for no particular reason whatsoever, I kept a few bottles (not even knowing what they were and intending to research them at a later time). This all happened a few months *prior* to my cancer diagnosis, and I had promptly forgotten the box with books and bottles that I had thrown in our garage. A week following my cancer diagnosis, while getting something out of the freezer in the garage, that box fell down off a shelf onto the floor at my feet. I took it as a message from the universe. I began to read the book and read all through that auspicious day into the next. The writer cited the use of a number of supplements unknown to me. I wondered where I'd ever find them.

Guess where? Every single one cited in that book was in that same box that fell off the shelf and into my lap that day. Remember, I didn't make any connections between the cancer book I had kept and the bottles of supplements I threw into the box weeks later. Even the fact that they were in the same box together was astounding to me. However, I didn't hesitate, not even for a moment. I just read the directions in the book and on the bottles, and I started taking them the very next day. I was four weeks away from my surgery date and had every hope that using them would help halt the ominous spread and strengthen my body for the big fight ahead. Talk about surrender and trust!

In addition to seeing my family physician and my team of oncologists, I also made appointments with a naturopath and a practitioner of Traditional Chinese Medicine (TCM). Like I said before, I would employ every means at my disposal to survive cancer, and I did. The naturopath put me on Reishi and Glutamine, both of which were immune system aides. The TCM doctor counseled me at length about the nature of my life from childhood to the present. In review and discussion of my life leading up to my cancer diagnosis, Dr G explained that the stresses I had lived through for so long kept me in a never-ending survival mode of fight, flight, or freeze. On a scale of 1 to 10, said Dr. G, he would rate me an unrelenting 10 or 12! I argued the point, saying that I imagined I had a good life. Despite challenges along the way, I had enjoyed many rewards throughout the years. However, the belief that I was happy denied the fact that I was actually alone and abandoned and unhappy. This repression of my pain was my essential survival adaptation. But we can become imprisoned in our adaptations.

Dr G spoke to me of life stressors that he deemed responsible for pre-empting disease in the body, and that the emotionally based coping mechanisms that get programmed into our brains in childhood often manifest as a diagnosis later in life. When authentic emotions aren't responded to by one's parents, (not because they don't love you but because they are too stressed), you shut down because it's too painful to have feelings that are not validated by the world.

This notion was later reiterated to me upon reading Dr. Gabor Maté's book, *When The Body Says No.* Maté cited that it wasn't the presence of life stressors and emotions such as anger and resentment in themselves that are the main source of illness, but **the repression of** those emotions over an extended period of time. In all of his cancer patient cases, unresolved conflicts manifested in unrealistic self-sacrificing behaviors and in an extreme suppression of feelings, which then magnified the patients' exposure to physiological stress. This was a common denominator among the psychological profiles of all of his patients. Every single one of them also shared the propensity to be highly productive and positive-minded people; People who took everything in stride, however severe the trauma, however intense the crisis. These people refused to allow life circumstances to take them down and were strong minded, strong hearted survivors one and all. Maté explains that stress is a physiological response to a *perceived* threat (physical *or* emotional), even if the person is unaware of that perception.

People in repression (in a lack of awareness of one's feelings, and also in the inability to say no) are more likely to find themselves in situations where one's emotions are unexpressed, needs are ignored, and their kindness and compassion are exploited. Maté explains that when these circumstances are repeated and multiplied over the years, they have the potential of harming homeostasis. Repression compromises the immune system and undermines a body's balance and immune defenses, which predisposes one to disease, and reduces a body's resistance to it. Repression is a coping mechanism, a self-preservation tool. Although it is a self-protective measure, it is a far cry from anything even faintly resembling self-love. Repression and self-love cannot exist in tandem. I recognized that at this point in my life I couldn't have even begun to define what self-love would look like. The concept was foreign to me.

After my initial consultation with my TCM doctor, which was 3.5 hours of counseling and a half hour of acupuncture, I was walking out of the door of his office that day, when Dr. G stopped me and asked, "Are you sure you want to stay with this man?"

His question shocked me. Shrugging away any concern I might have heard in his voice, I nonchalantly replied, "Yes of course. He's my husband."

Fast forward three years, and I would come to understand why Dr G had posed that question to me. You, too, will soon understand as my story unfolds in subsequent chapters.

During recovery I went into a kind of self-imposed isolation. I saw people go straight from their chemotherapy treatments back to work that same day, but I went home to bed. I wrote affirmations on poster paper and taped them in my direct line of vision onto the closet door in my bedroom (thank you Louise Hay). I felt fragile and sick, so I wrote, "I Am Strong and Healthy."

I felt disregarded, disrespected, undeserving, and somehow unworthy of love. More than any one other thing, *I felt so unloved.* And so I wrote, "I am loved."

I said those words every morning and every night for the next eighteen months of treatment. Even when I didn't believe them. The thing about affirmations is that your mind doesn't know that what you are saying isn't true for you at the time, but it begins to believe the words it is hearing, and the belief slowly but surely begins to shift...until the words become true for you. So, I dutifully chanted my affirmations over and over again.

And I cried. I cried a lot. Forty years worth of not crying came gushing out of me. Forty years of tears — I cried and cried and cried. Those tears became transcendent.

Somewhere deep down inside myself I knew that there were a multitude of reasons why I had come to feel so unloved and so unwell. They all involved the choices I made to put everyone's happiness before my own. As a family therapist, I put so much energy into helping others. As a wife and mother, I lived my life for my husband and my children. It didn't occur to me to explore this choice, it just felt like the way it was supposed to be. Moreover, the circumstance of living with a spouse with a serious mental illness (my husband was bi-polar) put me in survival mode much of the time. Living through the stresses his illness put our family through was the petri dish that my cancer grew in.

I believe the circumstances of his illness were the primary conditions by which I learned to cope with stress by repressing it, and that fed the petri dish that my cancer grew in. Every time his mania escalated into psychosis and he needed to be hospitalized, I would do everything in my power to make our lives appear 'normal' so as not to traumatize our children (even as I was frightened and often traumatized by the unpredictable circumstances of his bizarre behaviors).

Normalizing it kept me in pretense mode, pretending everything was okay, despite that it was *so* not. I was unintentionally modeling how to repress my very real emotions of fear, worry, resentment and anger. I don't mean to say that it was his illness, with the accompanying stresses wrought on our lives per se that contributed to my cancer. I am saying that my *repression of vital emotions and my own codependent responses* in reaction to what was happening in our lives were largely responsible. I would need to rebuild my capacity to feel.

We pay a price for living in chronic survival mode as our unresolved emotional pain becomes physical. I was often surprised when other people would sympathize with my circumstances as being so much more traumatic than I perceived them to be. I had learned to normalize my trauma and my suffering, my own and my family's dysfunctions, and in doing so somehow denied its credence. I had not allowed the experiences to throw me into chaos, and I thought that was good. I was coping. But I had completely disengaged to the degree that I was generating a superficial auto-pilot setting of survival. Not good. I was so afraid of my husband abandoning me and his family that I was doing everything in my power to try to fix him (Codependency 101!) Codependency isn't in the DSM (Diagnostic and Statistical Manual of Mental Disorders), but I believe it should be. In truth, he was doing just that (abandoning us) every single time he got sick and suffered another psychotic episode.

It took thirteen years for my husband to finally be diagnosed appropriately. Until then, we had little to go on in terms of understanding the nature of his illness. Once he had a clear diagnosis, I could finally do some research on all that was written about manic/depressive cycles, and their accompanying symptoms. It was such a relief to see documentation about all that he and we were living through. We finally had evidence that fit the picture! But every case is different, and my husband's cycles were unusual in that they only occurred every four to five years.

However far and few between, they were severe and lengthy. I documented each and every one in my journal, and it was this very documentation that eventually gave the doctors insight into his diagnosis.

One of my greatest frustrations throughout the years was in struggling to advocate for my ill husband while he, in delusion, was the one that entered the closed door of the psychiatrist's office, alone. His fear of being hospitalized and given medication that would bring him down from his high found him masking his symptoms to the best of his ability. More often than not he did a damn good job of it which inevitably postponed his hospitalization until such time as I would need to employ the intervention of the RCMP to get him to the psych ward. They would always enquire whether he was a danger to himself or to others. I always believed him to be more of a danger to himself than to anyone else (I was never afraid of him in this state), but I feared he would inadvertently hurt himself by jumping off the barn roof or something, believing he could fly! After every episode, it didn't take weeks or months for him to stabilize again, but literally years (usually 18 months to two years in the 'depressive' aspect of his cycle) before he could work again.

One of his most frightening episodes occurred long before he was diagnosed Bi-Polar. It was less than ten years into our marriage, and we had three young children, with the youngest under a year, still nursing and on the bottle. We were all in the family car driving home from the swimming pool when he took to the highway and decided we would travel from where we lived in the Okanagan to Vancouver on the Pacific Northwest coast (about a five-hour drive). He was wearing his farm chore rubber boots, and the children and I had only what we were wearing. I never traveled without a cooler full of food in the car, and suitcases packed for any eventuality. I tried to reason with him that we couldn't travel so unprepared, but he was charismatic and convincing in his argument that we could indeed have an unexpected family adventure, and why didn't I just relax and go with the flow, that everything was under control!

How could I not have understood how very out of control our lives were? Maybe I was fooling myself, believing I was not afraid during these unpredictable occasions, for I was very careful not to spark his ire, and I humbly succumbed to his wishes. We had under $20 in our pockets and purse, so I envisioned us stranded on the highway somewhere. This was the late 1980's, so cell phones weren't yet in common use. We made it to Vancouver and showed up on the doorstep of my brother who lived there. Surprisingly? Not really. My husband had this uncanny ability to inspire trust in his ability to do what was right and see us through any circumstance safely and soundly, no matter what.

And I did trust him to do so, regardless of his compromised state of mind. And most ironically, he never failed in that regard. So, however bizarre the circumstances we were in, I trusted him. Though maybe now in retrospect, I wonder if I didn't actually trust myself and the universe more than I did him. Upon arrival late in the evening, I tucked the kids into bed there, and I cried myself to sleep hoping a good night's sleep would find my husband stable enough that I could reason with him come morning.

The new day dawning always brought me hope, and when morning came, I was happy to usher the kids back into the car to go out for breakfast, and hopefully head back home. However, en route over the Lions Gate Bridge my husband pronounced he would take us all to heaven, saving us all from the suffering of life on earth. I knew then that it was his intention to purposely drive right off that bridge. I reprimanded him as a mother would a child and asked that he just listen to me long enough to get the kids some breakfast. But breakfast was the last thing on my mind at this point; I could only hope he would listen.

I closed my eyes to pray for protection and for help from God. It's strange how in crisis we fall back on age-old habits, and I found myself saying the Hail Mary's of my Catholic upbringing.

Then I felt prompted by Spirit to keep my eyes closed while giving my husband driving directions. This was blind faith at its best, and it sounds ridiculous, I know. I don't know why, but I obviously believed without a doubt in my own instincts for survival — and in divine intervention. For the next ten minutes I said things like, take the next left, go four blocks and take a right at the next set of lights. Soon, I asked him to turn into the next gas station, and to stop there. Against all odds, he listened to me. I opened my eyes, and I looked up. In front of us was a sign that said, "Emergency Medical Clinic." I would say my prayers were answered, wouldn't you?

I was somehow able to convince him to go into the clinic with me. Though he did everything in his power to convince the staff there that it was I that needed intervention, the doctor immediately recognized that he was in a state of psychosis and admitted him to hospital. We remained in Vancouver for another 10 days while my husband recovered in hospital.

This wasn't the first time he had this kind of episode, and I suspected it wouldn't be the last. Consequently, the upheaval and stress of uncertainty and the emotional trauma I felt was pretty much constant, and *super vigilance* became my mode of transportation through life. It began to make sense to me that the near *constant state of fight or flight could be* the basis for which my cancer and my RA bred itself into existence in my body. When reading Glenon Doyle's book, *Untamed*, the lines that would strike me most profoundly would be that I would need to shift from, "How could he have done this to me?" to "How could I have done this to myself?" and from, "How could he have abandoned me?" to "Why do I keep abandoning myself?"

That ownership, of taking responsibility for where I was at this moment in time, was absolutely essential. It was nobody else's fault, and nobody else could fix it but me.

Chapter 4

Denial to Divorce

It was during the time of treatment and recovery from cancer that I made the decision to end my forty year marriage. I had contemplated the question so many times throughout those four decades, so why now? It wasn't the Stage 4 cancer diagnosis per se, but it was during the aftermath of treatment that I began to understand that there could be no other way if I wanted to survive. For, although I was familiar with feeling abandoned by him, never was it more apparent than over those 18 months of chemotherapy and radiation treatment when, despite feeling frail and frightened, I still refused to believe he could abandon me in this my greatest time of need.

Yet, he did. I had asked that he not share my bedroom at this time as I was awake at all hours of the night, restless and uncomfortable. He honored my request, but neither did he ever set foot in there again. He never sat by my bedside and held my hand. He never held me in his arms to bring me comfort. He rarely even drove me to appointments when I couldn't drive myself.

Why was I so surprised that he wasn't there for me? He had rarely ever been before, and now I was twenty pounds heavier and bald! I aged 20 years in those 18 months, and he was unable to see me beyond my flesh and bones. Had he ever, I wondered?

If the important values of marriage are honesty, faithfulness, and loyalty, which of these could I count on to see us through this time around? I had already crossed off honesty as the poor man struggled to tell the truth even on the most trivial of matters, but because I could see through him every single time it became a moot point. We even laughed about it more often than not. Sadly, he was unable to keep his vow of faithfulness, as well, when he had an affair with a woman 30 years younger. But because she lived in Cuba where he worked for a number of years, I found hope for reconciliation of our marriage when he quit his job there. Now the absence of loyalty to me while I was sick destroyed my last hope. Without any of those values intact, it was time to face the music. It was time to move on, and I had finally found the incentive and the courage to take action.

I wondered if it was never my intention to do anything but love him, did it mean that I had failed when 40 years later I couldn't love him anymore? It certainly felt like failure, in as much as I always believed in positive outcomes, and I failed to make one happen for the two of us. It felt like failure in the way that I was hurting knowing I had to give up on us. It felt like failure in feeling so much anger toward myself for staying for so long, for trying so damn hard to fix it — to no avail. And it felt like failure when I recognized that the subservience I had called devotion for all the years I strived to be a good wife and a good mother (that felt so honorable at the time) had turned what I believed to be a virtue into a vice.

I had become so well practiced at denial it was difficult to break that particular pattern. I was in denial thinking that I had been giving my all with no expectations for being given anything in return. Wasn't I just such a god damn martyr? After all, wasn't it less than honorable to want or need or ask for anything for myself, or to imagine my needs were even valid than to meet the needs of others? It simply became habitual to imagine instead that I must be doing something wrong, that I was undeserving and unworthy. It must be my fault. I was the one feeling stranded and alone in a relationship and in a life that was supposed to be all about togetherness as a couple and as a family, while my husband, on the other hand, professed he was perfectly happy.

I believe he was indeed very happy within the confines of our marriage. If I was good at anything, it would have been to dispense tender loving care to those I loved. And I remained demonstrative throughout our marriage.

Moreover, Bob expressed to me early in our relationship that he had never known a mother's love. In some ways, I think I fulfilled that role for him, often nurturing him with praise and heartfelt gestures of admiration as a mother might. And I may very well have seen him in somewhat of a father's role, as well. My father had abandoned his family when I was ten years of age. We definitely assumed old fashioned roles: he the breadwinner; I the homemaker and child rearer while he worked away. We were both more than comfortable and accepting of these roles.

Of the three levels of intimacy that it's important to meet in an intimate relationship (physical, emotional, and intellectual), I think we had two out of three of them well covered in our early years together. We were intellectually compatible, physically passionate, and even emotionally supportive some of the time. As the years went by and he worked away longer and longer stretches of time, I would begin to feel a huge lack of the emotional support I so craved. But in the beginning, I felt like all my needs and desires were being met. When we first dated, we spent hours and hours talking about our plans for the future. We dreamed our dreams aloud and marveled at the similarities between them.

We all know that our childhoods shape who we become as adults. As the eldest of eight children in a family living in poverty (with an alcoholic father and a mentally ill mother), Bob had assumed a patriarchal role at the tender age of 14 when he left school and home to go work on the railroad. He took such pride in the exemplary work ethic that he had honed very early in his life. His work truly consumed him. I was proud of my hardworking man.

Though I wanted to blame him for not being able to love me, deep down in the confines of my heart (where I tucked away the pain of rejection so no one else might guess it was there) I blamed myself for not being good enough. Otherwise, why would I choose to stay in dysfunction and pain? Why did I imagine I could fix the man in his illness, the marriage, the relationship, the broken dreams? It never occurred to me then that I had to face fixing myself. After all, it was *me* that allowed myself to be mistreated that way. I was too stubborn, too self-righteous, too fearful, and completely unaware of how fiercely codependent I had become.

Ultimately, codependence is about an attempt at having something under one's control when all else in life feels so damn convoluted and out of control. It's the darndest thing because the well-practiced codependent really and truly believes they are acting in everybody's best interest. Their behaviors are terribly controlling but delivered with such heartfelt good intention they truly can't imagine that they are doing anything wrong. They have no conception of boundaries whatsoever.

Breaking my lifelong pattern of deeply instilled codependency was one of the tools I would need to strap on my tool-belt when I finally hit the open road to freedom. Melody Beattie's, *Codependent No More,* and, *The Language of Letting Go*, would help me greatly in that regard. I learned that underneath the trauma that the dysfunction wrought were patterns of behavior and beliefs about the world that I had learned in childhood. At some point I would need to revisit occasions from my childhood where my memories reside and relive the memory again as the little girl feeling the feelings that my younger self felt.

My first experience uncovering some of these unconscious beliefs occurred in an online Mindvalley Masterclass with Marisa Peer. While in a rapid transformational hypnosis therapy session, I regressed back to my childhood to an incident I remembered at about age 10. I remembered asking my mother if I could have a new set of school clothes because I only had one outfit to wear to school all week while my peers wore a different outfit every day. My school outfit was a Canadian tartan kilt and a white blouse that I could change up by wearing a brown cardigan or black fishnet stockings. We had recently moved to the city of Edmonton from a small town in the interior of BC where I attended a Catholic school, in uniform. So, it didn't feel weird for me to wear the same thing to school every day until my peers pointed it out. My mother was a single parent of five children receiving no spousal or child support from her absent husband. She apologetically replied that she couldn't afford to buy me anything new, and that I would need to earn my own money to do so. She went on to explain that as the eldest daughter with three younger siblings, it was my responsibility to take care of them while she was at work, while my older brother at age fourteen was already working after school and on weekends, bringing his paycheck home to help her make ends meet financially. I proudly took on the helping role she asked of me. Did I resent it? I may have, but because I don't recall having done so, I imagine I began repressing my uncomfortable and/or negative emotions at that very early age. I wouldn't have wanted to be seen as selfish or self-centered. I was a very devout young Catholic girl who wanted to be seen as humble and kind.

A number of simple, self-limiting beliefs can form in the mind of a growing young girl. *It's futile to ask for what you want. It's selfish and unwarranted. I am undeserving. Money is hard to come by, you must struggle to earn your keep. Always put others before yourself.*

This was in fact the second time I had heard a similar message, so it was certainly becoming embedded within my psyche. I recalled one incident of my childhood even more vividly as it was a celebratory occasion — my 5th or maybe my 6th birthday. One of the guests arrived at the door, and I greeted her in anticipation of another present, but she didn't have one for me. I turned to my mother with disappointment saying, "She didn't bring me a present mommy!" My mother promptly reprimanded me exclaiming, "It is *not* nice to say that, Charlotte! Her friendship is the best gift of all, and you should never expect anything more. Don't be selfish and ungrateful when you already have so much." What did I learn? Don't ask for what you want. It is selfish and wrong to have desires of your own." Maybe in my very young mind the words I heard may even have translated to mean *wanting something for yourself makes you a bad person.* These self-limiting beliefs that I had gathered in childhood stayed with me throughout my whole life, and they set the stage for the self-sabotaging behaviors I assumed throughout my marriage.

During those many long hours I spent resting in bed during my cancer treatment and recovery, I was enjoying my privacy and found I began to cherish my solitude. This made the notion of ending my marriage a less fearful one. Maybe I didn't have to keep trying so hard to make it work all by myself. I was actually ready to share the burden of expectations, admitting to myself that it would take two committed people to make a marriage work, and it would need recognition of a *need* for change by both people. However, that was only ever **my** agenda, not his. He was perfectly happy living life on his own terms. He professed to me that *he* was *happy.* How could I find fault in that, when all the guru's profess that you must love yourself first before you can love anyone else? He had that one down pat. Furthermore, he could be rightfully excused, for he had a bona-fide diagnosis of a long standing mental illness, and I was advised by professionals that I must learn to cope on the premise that I needed to separate the man from the illness. In other words, if when in the throes of mania or psychosis he was cruel, or emotionally abusive, or narcissistic and arrogant, well it just wasn't his fault.

One day it occurred to me that I may have married the *potential* I had seen in him, that the man I had fallen in love with, the man I believed had integrity and honor, the man who expressed that he wanted to be a good husband and a good father (who wanted to break the patterns of abuse and alcoholism that he grew up with), *was gone.* That I hadn't seen him for a very long time. I tried for years to find him again, and to inspire his return, but I finally just got tired, so very, very tired. I felt completely depleted. I felt completely emptied of all my strength and perseverance. My body got sick, and my heart gave up. I absolutely could not put one more breath of effort into searching for a man I once knew that had gone away and wasn't coming back.

The straw that broke the camel's back for me was when, one last time before the big step forward, I asked him, "Do you want to try to save our marriage, or do you want a divorce?"

"I don't have to divorce you," he replied, "I just have to wait you out because you'll be dead in a couple of years anyway."

My reply came with a vengeance (like a promise to myself).

"I'll outlive you, just wait and see!"

And so, with both relief and a kind of tentative hope, I also felt a deep sadness and cried more tears on the day I filed for divorce. Because the loss of a love is no less painful than the loss of a life. And we must grieve.

Chapter 5

Keeping Vigil

DURING THE FIRST YEAR FOLLOWING MY OWN CANCER TREATMENTS, my sister was diagnosed with lung Cancer. Her diagnosis was Small Cell Carcinoma, and it was terminal. I was diagnosed in the spring of 2016, and she in the winter of 2018. Despite her terminal diagnosis, she was hopeful. She saw that I had beaten it, as had so many others, and she believed she could, too. But she deteriorated very quickly, and she simply couldn't find the strength within her to take up arms in battle against it. She had battled with clinical depression for many years, and she was feeling generally defeated by life. Life had been a rather constant struggle for her over the past twenty years and she had weathered much of it in solitude. She had a strong group of friends that loved her dearly, and siblings and nieces and nephews that were there for her, but still she felt alone in the world. A part of me believes she chose to leave this hard old world behind to greet her mother and her brother in the spirit realm.

During her first appointment with her team of oncologists, she was told she only had six weeks to live. She survived nearly six months longer out of sheer will and lived in the joy of feeling showered with love during that time. I spent three of those months living with her in hospice. It kind of felt like old times sharing an apartment in our youth — talking, laughing, reminiscing, listening to good music, and eating really good food (everything her heart desired).

It was during this time, when I would return home to another province to be with my husband, that I would come to realize that I was happier sitting at my dying sister's bedside than I was coming home to him. Soon after she died, I began the process of filing for divorce. Because we had been living separately for many months already, the legal time of separation required before the divorce could be finalized was shortened considerably, and six months later, in February of 2019, I was suddenly divorced!

Four short months later, in June of that self-same year, my (ex) husband would be diagnosed with lung cancer, too. A year later (almost to the day of first being diagnosed), he passed.

"He just couldn't live without me," I joked. But, I believe he really couldn't live without me taking care of him.

The year of his cancer journey was a traumatic one, both for him and for me. Post divorce, he had become terribly bitter, cruel and abusive. His anger consumed him, and he was drinking excessively morning to night, sabotaging all that he had once held dear to him. Even while in the depths of grief both for my sister's death and for the death of my 40-year marriage, I felt a deep compassion toward him. From my perspective, he was just so very ill. Bi-polar disorder, alcoholism, and now he was dealing with cancer. I could understand why he was so angry.

Much of his anger was most probably felt at a deep unconscious level towards himself. Although he had little justification to do so, he placed all the blame and directed all his anger toward me. He had to direct it somewhere.

Which brings me to the part of the story I really don't want to tell. I struggle with the telling. My heart beats faster, I feel that uncomfortable rush of adrenaline pumping through my veins, and I don't want to say the words. I don't want to dig the dirt out from underneath the carpet, or to open the door to this particular closet! If not for Isabella Braveheart's online five-day challenge of embodied storytelling, I wouldn't be writing it. Watching countless other women speak their truths (many of their stories much more horrendous than mine) with tears streaming down their faces, I am now compelled to include it, knowing how integral it is to the healing process, to find the courage to break the silence.

For the first time in our forty years together, I was afraid of my (ex) husband. As you now know, I had seen him in and out of psychotic episodes that were frightening in the degree of delusion he was suffering, but never once in all that time had I felt myself to be in danger in his presence. Now I did. I was scared from a deep place of knowing within me (beyond conscious reasoning) as I accepted a message from Spirit that was loud and clear. *He wants to hurt me.*

Despite our divorce we both continued to live on the same property but in different residences. Having lived on our ten-acre hobby farm for the past 30 years, we had yet to resolve a division of property, because we promised we would never sell it, and it would remain in the family as a legacy for our grandchildren. It had always felt like a safe and sacred place, and never once in all those years had I ever locked my doors. But I began to do so, both night and day, even when at home. I didn't know how or what he might do, but I felt a deep sense of foreboding that if given the opportunity, when I least expected it, he would attempt to harm me.

I thought about how so many of his circumstances had changed. I think he felt abandoned by me, even though I continued to be there for him in many ways — to cook him a meal or buy him groceries. But I was no longer there to comfort and soothe him, and no longer there to validate and support him. And though drinking the pain away is as valid a coping mechanism as any other in the scheme of things, it only works until it doesn't. And it had stopped working for him. Though he continued to be falling down drunk by noon every day, it was no longer working to keep his demons at bay.

As far as he was concerned, it was all my fault. So, my due diligence being hyper vigilant had always served me well in the past, and I expected that it would do so once again. My best coping mechanism was to keep busy, and my kitchen was my favorite place for productivity.

That day I was making lasagna. My cupboards were lined with 6 or 7 large pans waiting to be filled with all the ingredients I had been prepping all morning. I had gone next door to my daughter's place to borrow something and upon return I forgot to re-lock my kitchen door. My back was turned away from the door as I began layering the pans with meat sauce and noodles, and ricotta and spinach. I was intent on my task. He came silently up behind me and clasped his arms around my middle.

"I'm going to rape you bitch!" he whispered in my ear in a sinister voice I had never heard before.

My old methods of persuasion to reason with him when he was in delusion kicked in, and I expected they would work as they often did before. I made light of what was happening, pretending to laugh.

"Don't be ridiculous," I announced. "I'm in the middle of cooking here! Sit down, and I'll make you a coffee and we can talk."

I pleaded. I squirmed out from under his grasp, turned around and saw his eyes. That is when I got more scared than I had ever been, for I had never seen eyes that held that much disdain and evil intention. They were certainly not the eyes of my husband,

and I knew those eyes well after forty years. I had fallen in love with those eyes once upon a time.

He grabbed me again as I frantically scanned the area looking for my phone, and he repeated his threat.

"I said, I'm going to rape you, and then I'm going to kill you, bitch!"

I didn't know where he was finding the strength to hold me. It was past noon, and by this time of day he could barely stand up let alone fight. But his strength prevailed, and it took all I had in me to fight back. Finally getting away from him and running to the back door, grabbing my phone from the counter on my way, I dialed 911 while running out of the door.

When I reached the steps of my daughter's house (where my son in law was asleep as he had worked a night shift), I glanced back, wondering if my husband was still in pursuit, but he wasn't. He was ambling slowly back to his trailer in the yard. Still, though the threat was no longer upon me I was shaking so badly I could hardly hold the phone as I relayed to the RCMP the events that had just unfolded.

He was taken to jail overnight while I called a friend for support, staying with her overnight in fear that he would return home. The next day an RCMP officer came to record another statement from me. He explained that my husband was in such rough shape physically, he was taken to the local hospital for observation. He added that the physician on call that morning said that the man's organs were shutting down due to alcohol poisoning, and he would be admitted for further tests. I spoke with the RCMP every day in fear of his being discharged from hospital and coming back home.

While there, further tests revealed that he had advanced lung cancer. If he was angry before, I imagined this prognosis would only escalate his anger and resentment toward me. I had survived, and he might not. When he was asked by a family member what his dying wish would be should he not survive, he replied, "That that bitch dies before I do!"

Consequently, the RCMP advised that upon his discharge from hospital, I should get the hell out of town. So, I did. I was running for my life.

I stayed away for almost a month. I felt pretty messed up inside, but as time went on, I began to diminish the severity of the incident. As part of the retribution claim, I was allotted 24 counseling sessions which I welcomed wholeheartedly, and my therapist helped me to understand that it wasn't uncommon for someone whose life was fraught with trauma and crisis to normalize it to the degree that I did. In other words, it didn't seem all that bad after a while. It seemed somewhat normal. During my time away, I was in constant communication with the RCMP's crime victims support team, and they finally gave me the go ahead to return home. My husband was issued a restraining order to stay away from me and our property. But you can bet I continued to lock my door!

Even though safety measures were in place, I remained on guard until he left town to live with his sister in Alberta. I don't really know what the nature of his lies were about me, but over the next few months he managed to solicit the sympathy of all his friends and family, including our own children who turned away from me. Though I had sought their approval my whole live-long life, this time around it just didn't matter anymore.

I couldn't have done anything differently. I couldn't have disregarded his gaslighting disdain and judgment if I tried. It wasn't merely a feeling anymore. I really was abandoned by those that I loved. And though it hurt me more deeply than anything, for the first time ever I didn't let it matter. I couldn't let it matter. This moment in time was my first lesson in self-love. Even standing more alone than I had ever been, even with tears streaming down my face, I felt loved! Because I had chosen 'me.'

As my husband's condition worsened, he had been doing relatively well keeping the cancer wolves at bay while using CBD oil. He began supplementing that with THC as an alternative to morphine, and he immediately went into mania followed by deep psychosis. During that time, as his cancer metastasized further and spread into his brain, he spent the next three months in the psychiatric ward of the local hospital. Having seen him there many times before didn't make it any easier, it made it seem worse, as it was obvious that these were to be the last months of his life.

When he returned home for three short months following his stay in the psych ward, he would come to terms with the fact that he was dying. Though the restraining order against him for threatening my life remained in place, I worked to have it lifted, and I welcomed him back into my home on the same farm we had lived on together for the past thirty years. The farm was meant to be our legacy to our grandchildren when we died. He always called our little ten-acre hobby farm sacred land. *This* was where he wanted to be when he died, and *I* was who he wanted to be holding his hand. Despite everything that had come to pass, he was no longer a threat to me, and I could feel compassion for a tired and broken dying man. I wanted to fulfill his final request.

I never regretted that decision. Before I firmly made that decision, I asked the universe for a sign. I wanted something more than just my own instinct to tell me whether that particular decision of mine would be a good one; right or wrong I needed a sign. The day after posing that prayer, on a sunny summer morning when both my front and back doors were opened to the beautiful day, a Red-Tailed Hawk flew right into my house. It landed on a windowsill and sat there calmly for the next 15 minutes before I awoke my grandson and asked him to gently pick the bird up and put it back outside. You can't make this stuff up! Had the bird flapped furiously around, frantically trying to escape, I would have taken the message to be an adamant, 'No.' The whole experience felt so beautifully spiritual that I considered it a loud and clear, 'Yes.'

There's a bit of a background story here. Before my brother passed away in 1994, I asked that he give me a 'sign' that there was life after death and that the soul continues on its journey. At the memorial we held for him in a community hall, a blue jay flew into the hall when the song I had chosen to play for him was playing. It landed on the speaker, then flew over and landed on my head (atop the cowboy hat I was wearing, which was his). It stayed there throughout the whole song before it made its way over to the buffet table where it picked away at the dill pickles on a platter. If Rand was there in body rather than spirit, he would have commented that the dill pickles needed more salt! Everyone present agreed he was definitely there in spirit in the body of that beautiful mountain blue jay. So, when my sister's death was looking imminent, I asked her what kind of bird she was going to be.

"Maybe a dove?" I asked.

"Hell no," she replied. "That's way too woosy! Maybe a hawk."

So, despite the drama and the trauma that unfolded that year, I never regretted the decision to invite my ex-husband to be at home on the farm and under my roof. God and the universe (plus the spirit of my sister in the form of a hawk) were telling me it was going to be okay.

The aftermath of death has a way of suspending you. You feel somewhat tugged up and away from the earth as though accompanying the departed soul. As the caregiver of the dying person, you accompany them each step of the way to the threshold of departure, half in and half out of the reality that still binds them to the earth. For days, weeks, and months following, you sometimes second guess the nature of that final time spent together, as I did. I questioned what I might have done differently during those final weeks. I questioned how I might have brought him more comfort. I struggled to understand my part in it all, and I mourned that I didn't have it in me to give him my love. I regret not having been able to say, "I love you," in the way that he wanted to hear it. I could nourish him with food and drink to take care of his mortal needs and grant him companionship, but I was hesitant and resistant to express sincere affection for him. I could say, "You are so loved," but forgiveness isn't necessarily accompanied with a renewal of love and devotion. I couldn't say the words that later I would realize didn't have to be said because *he* deserved them, but *because everyone does. Everybody deserves* to leave this world on the wings of all the love they garnered in their time on earth. I just felt sad knowing I couldn't have done it any differently. Later, I would learn that *unconditional love* meant that you could love without attachment. So, I could have given him my unconditional love, but I was yet to learn *that* lesson. I was yet to learn that we are one and all loved unconditionally, just because.

Chapter 6

Grief and Loss

I DON'T THINK I EVER TRULY BELIEVED THE DAY WOULD COME that I could and would fulfill my promise to be holding his hand as he left this world, yet I had kept vigil at his bedside, and had given him all that I could give him in his final weeks. I said all the words that I needed to say, as I believe he did as well, to some extent. We shared some happy memories, some tears, and some semblance of forgiveness.

The idiosyncrasies of forgiveness would be something I would revisit time and again over the next many months. I would learn that *forgiveness is an essential step in moving forward, but moreover that it is not for the benefit of the other person at all, but for oneself.*

I would remember the vows we took on a snowy December evening in a little country church (walking down the aisle to *Silent Night*), and I realized with pride and joy that I had fulfilled them to the end, till, "Death do us part."

His siblings and his children and his grandchildren gathered together and gave him their love and bade him goodbye with tenderness and honor. And he was glad.

He asked that there be no memorial but had heard of the tradition of the sacred fire, and being of First Nations heritage, he liked that idea. The fire we built for him on the day of his passing burned, smoldered, and flamed for five days and five nights until his body was laid to rest, and his spirit set free. I know he smiled down upon us as we welcomed friends and family to honor and celebrate his life by throwing a log on the fire in his memory. On those days, it rained and rained, and the thunder rolled, and the lightning flashed, and the clouds parted to reveal a brilliant blue sky slashed with sunshine, and a rainbow rising over the crest of the hills. The grass appeared greener than green, and the salt of our tears mingled with the memories of a man that was loved despite himself. Some of the pain of the past dispersed with the sacred smoke drifting up into the heavens and over the land he held in his heart and called home.

Children are so beautifully instinctive. My granddaughter poured a little Pepsi onto the fire, proclaiming, "I'm giving Grandpa a drink, it's his favorite."

When dawn came early on the rainy night that I helped tend the fire to keep the embers glowing, I went into the house to brew myself a coffee, and in doing so, it occurred to me that Bob would like one too, so I fixed one for him the way that he liked it (black, one sugar), lit a cigarette to go with it, and placed them both on a stump by the fire till the cigarette burned down to the filter, before finally throwing them both into the flames.

My grandson fed the fire a piece of his fry bread (another favorite of Grandpa's which I made for friends dropping by). The burning of some of his clothes and belongings, the offering of his favorite foods, all were prior to finding out that these were indeed traditions associated with the sacred fire ritual practiced by First Nations Peoples. It occurred to me that ritual is a form of prayer (so much of it instinctual) and that *sacred practices are imminently important to our healing. There was indeed a sense of closure as day unfolded into night for those five days.*

In the days and weeks that followed, my grief felt familiar for I had grieved the loss of love before, but I never imagined that nostalgia could be so acute or the memories of better days long ago so poignant —how my head fit perfectly into the crook of his shoulder blade when we were young and in love, or how my big boned hands felt safe and small in his protective grip. Even when he worked far away as he so often did, the children and I always felt the strength of his protective spirit.

Grief got twisted up inside sometimes. It remembered the twisted feelings of having loved someone who mistreated me, who turned away from me time and again while I struggled to separate the man from his illness. It remembered how hard I worked to hold things together — a family, a farm, a marriage — when he went off the rails flying free, battling his demons, and even battling the angels that somehow watched over him and brought him back to earth time and again, exhausted and spent in more ways than one. He came back every time, but he came back even more deeply wounded.

I have always loved the quote, "The dark places inside us are not where we are bad, but where we are wounded." His pride so often overrode his humility, and the tenderness he felt that was too deep to show its face behind his prideful eyes. Yet, in the end, he struggled to let them surface in remorse and tearful regret. They surfaced in desperation to come full circle before the gates of heaven claimed him.

Nearing the end, he confessed to me that he knew his misery was self-inflicted, his blame misguided, his anger and his pain a self-fulfilled prophecy of guilt and shame. He had allowed his dark side to defeat the light of love…until he came home again to find his peace and until he came home to himself. The gates of heaven opened in light and love, released him of his earthly pain and suffering, embraced his weary soul, and set him free.

This final farewell to the man I spent most of my life with would also be the truly final chapter of a part of my life I would have to learn to reconcile and leave behind. In order to heal, I would need to learn the real meaning of *letting go*.

Chapter 7

Letting Go

ESSENTIALLY, I HAD FINALLY TAKEN RESPONSIBILITY FOR THE choices I had made that brought me to where I was today. In doing so, I needed to forgive myself for all the ways I failed and self-sabotaged. Being unaware of doing so feels rather irrelevant at this point. I've never liked endings; the end of a good movie or a good book where the characters have become so familiar that they feel like family, when their stories reflect my own, or their hopes and their dreams mirror my own heartfelt longings. Yet when I turn the last page, or watch the credits roll, I know I'll find a new story tomorrow. Hope is a sturdy stepping stone.

I now realized I had spent many years in the self-made story I chose to live, only to find out how little the real me had in common with the character and the part I played. Yet, all those parts of that character became familiar enough to make me imagine she was real. As I ventured forth with hope and trepidation, I felt so grateful that I had come this far. I thanked God and the universe that part of my story had ended and that I had consciously turned the last page. I believed I could still find my happily ever after in which the 'real' me would come to life in a brand-new chapter.

That summer passed unaware, and as fall began to settle into the deep dark cold of a Canadian winter, I would truly begin the healing journey that would help me find my way home to myself. I realized that I had braved a wilderness of woe through the death of loved ones, the ravages of cancer and a divorce. I was feeling fragile and vulnerable in the pain of it all. My body, my heart, my very soul was screaming out in pain. That winter would indeed become the dark night of my soul.

This year from hell would become the most spiritually awakening time for me. Even as I traversed through the darkness, even when it felt scary or crazy making, something inside of me told me that I would be traveling toward the light of understanding, an ascension and a true rebirth of my soul self. Though sometimes messy and often intense, I knew that surrendering into the present moment of whatever I was feeling was the only way to get through it.

There is absolutely no way around the present; you must go through it. Renowned poet Robert Frost said, "The best way out is always through." Being willing to be in it, however uncomfortable, allowed me to move forward. Eventually I learned to make peace with what I was feeling, seeing and experiencing. I needed to believe that I was not broken, despite pain in my body and emotional scars from the past.

I had sheltered in place, and the casualty had been that of my heart in a million little pieces around me. And yet through it all I had hope. I could feel myself beginning to mend, as surely as a scab forms over an open wound, only to get smaller and smaller every time you rip it off. I ripped that scab off over and over again. On New Year's Eve of that year, I went out with a group of friends, and saying goodbye to the old year while welcoming in a new one was more nostalgic than ever before. I danced to the beat of an old rock and roll song, the words reverberating in my head. Fleetwood Mac's words reminded me to stop thinking about tomorrow that yesterday was gone. As the clock struck midnight and good wishes were handed out with hugs and kisses, I struggled to hold back my tears. I wasn't feeling sad. I wasn't feeling worried or stressed or uncomfortable. I was just feeling fragile. I prayed for the strength of heart to stop thinking about yesterday and to welcome tomorrow wholeheartedly.

I could begin to move forward in life, but not until I had learned what letting go really meant. When we are suffering, we are holding on really tightly. We are in strong control mode. The last thing we want to do when we are fearful or confused is to let go of what we imagine is in our control. Yet, very little in life is truly within our control, and the more we move toward acceptance of life circumstances, the less we suffer. We need to loosen our grip. But the idea that "she's lost her grip" has always been perceived as a bad thing. Still, the inner, heartfelt process of surrendering and easing up on our grip is intrinsic to waking up to the possibility of knowing we can be healed. Surrendering doesn't mean resigning ourselves or avoiding what's going on. In accepting all that our suffering entails, we are consciously letting go of the accompanying distress that the situation has wrought. When we let go of the controller within us, we say yes to allowing life to unfold as it will. A simpler way of saying it might be in the Alcoholic's Anonymous phrase, "Let go and let God."

My first experience with consciously choosing surrender came with my cancer diagnosis. Though I was eager to do whatever I could to fight the good fight, I also felt a deep sense of giving up to the support of something sacred — of Spirit. In that sense, I surrendered to my plight. I *surrendered my fear* of the outcome.

There are so many aspects of letting go, and the first is to surrender our resistance to it. What we resist persists! The second part of letting go is to surrender our identity as a fearful, unworthy, or deficit self who couldn't fix life's issues, or wasn't good enough. We must let go of the whole notion of being a failure and of having failed. The one regret that most people on their deathbed express is that they lived a life striving to live up to what they imagined was expected of them. They mistakenly expected certain things of themselves based on a self-limiting belief that they *should* be doing things a particular way. Their regret is based on having failed to find and to live *their own truth.*

My experience with this step came with the decision to go ahead with divorce. I first had to let go of the notion that I had failed. I believed I had failed to fix my marriage. I believed I had failed my children even though I stayed so long and imagining it was somehow for their sake. I believed I had failed in my decision 'to save the farm' as a legacy for my grandchildren when I could have left and forced the sale of the land, freeing us both to find new futures. I had to let go of all of these perceived failures and trust that it had all unfolded exactly as it was meant to, and trust that life always will, ensuring that all would be well in the end.

Fast forward a couple of years, and the Universe would show me that my ex-husband's death would validate my choices as having been sound ones all along. But I could very well have found myself on my own deathbed with the same regret so many others had expressed, for I *did* give myself away and fail to live my own truth for the longest time. Thankfully, awakened to the awareness of Spirit within me and beyond me, I began to find deeper meaning in life, however late in my life it was. Surrendering had taken me in two directions: to release the fear and to allow the faith. Letting go wasn't to deny the fear but to give it a voice and then let it pass through you and away. Every time you let go of something you make room for something new. When I let go of my fear, faith took its place, and then life felt complete.

A third step in surrendering is in *letting go of our thoughts* and the great influence they have on so many of our choices. We speak about losing our minds in the same way we speak about losing our grip — as though it's a negative thing. Thoughts are the vocabulary of our brain while emotions are the vocabulary of our body. Everything we think and feel defines our state of being.

We affirm the same state of being by continuing to think and feel the experiences of the past, therefore creating the self-same present and future. Somehow, the past continues to look through our eyes into our present and into our future. We all carry much ancestral karma and childhood conditioning around with us, we start believing this is who we are. But we can outgrow our old stories. We can grow. We can change. We get stuck by not being able to think greater than we feel. This familiarity of emotion keeps us stuck in what is best known to us, because the known always feels safer than the unknown. Change comes with making a new choice to think and feel differently, but doing so will always feel uncomfortable because we become conditioned to feeling the comfort of the familiar (however self-defeating that familiar is). We always want to fall back into what feels right in its familiarity.

We need to become aware of when that happens, for that first step of awareness is essential for us to be able to respond differently, and say, "No, this is not right, it's just familiar!"

We need to take the time to install new circuits into our brain, that most powerful organ resting in the head upon our shoulders. First, we need to develop the awareness of our memorized unconscious behaviors and patterns of the past, and of our emotions so that we can truly change. It is said that every person who has overcome some obstacle has overcome themselves, and that going from an old self to a new self is a neurological, biological, conscientious shift.

We do indeed have the capacity and the resources within us to recreate the circumstances of our lives, but if we are unwilling to go through the mud and the mire of facing our old self-defeating selves, we are unlikely to find the road paved to a brighter future. Chop wood, carry water. Do the work!

We begin by taking that long, hard look into the mirror to generate new awareness of exactly who we are, how we think, what we feel, how we act in any given moment on any given day. How? By staying curious and asking yourself questions then listening to the answers that arise out of your experience.

Meditation is a wonderful tool to use as a conscious way of letting go of our thoughts. My first attempts at meditation were nothing less than exacerbating. I couldn't for the life of me clear my monkey mind of its incessant meanderings. Into the stillness I could go, but into the emptiness was futile. So, I started with guided meditations. I found some that resonated deeply for me and practiced those few until they became automatic. Later, I learned that virtually everybody suffers the same frustration I experienced attempting to empty my mind, and that in itself is the whole point. Meditation is the practice of catching oneself in mid-thought and pulling oneself back into the quietude and stillness over and over again until it begins to work better and better. You repeat this practice until you eventually gain some mastery over yourself and your monkey mind.

I remember well the first time I achieved a true meditative state without intention, and I remember the wonder I felt. I had been practicing for almost three years at the time. I awoke very early on a cold winter morning, the only light in the room cast from the flames of the fire in the wood stove in my living room. The remnants of sleep still clung to me, and I knew this to be a particularly effective state to be in (Theta). Knowing I wouldn't be able to fall back asleep, I resolved to use this time to do a favorite healing meditation of mine. It is the old version of the microcosmic orbit (or small universe as it is called in Spring Forest Qigong).

I was in recovery from a hip replacement surgery and in a significant degree of pain. I put a log on the fire and sat in my favorite recliner. I knew the meditation was around 45 minutes long, yet hearing it wind down to the end I opened my eyes and glanced at the clock…and three hours had passed! Somehow between 5:30 am, and 8:45 AM I went into the emptiness void of thought. I knew I had not fallen back asleep for I remember the light slowly seeping into the sky as the darkness lifted, and I remember the deep abiding feeling of peace that enveloped me. I noticed that my pain was greatly diminished, for it was the time of day I would have generally reached for pain medication. Instead, I simply sat in wonder, feeling somehow suspended between heaven and earth. This had never happened before (despite all good intentions and concentrated efforts), and it might never happen again, but I would bow my head in gratitude for this moment etched in time when I felt touched by grace.

Meditation creates more space in the mind, so you can step back and become the observer. The lucid self becomes aware that your mind is moving, that the world is spinning, but it is all something you are watching. If we can separate who we are from our thoughts, we can become the one who sees…the seer. The intensity of our emotions also decreases in meditation, and your mind feels lighter. Intuition emerges, appearing as a calm, underlying knowing, like an inner compass that brings insight and clarity. Those insights can carry you through your day in observer mode so that you can even begin to see your own reaction to things without falling into an old pattern of behavior. We begin reframing by questioning our first reaction and deciding to react differently this time. In meditation you are the observer and the seer. Mediation is good medicine.

Stepping out of our heads in any way we can is an essential step in living in a purer state of consciousness. The way to understand that we are spiritual beings is to know that we are not all of the thoughts that are constantly swirling around in our heads all day long. When we step outside of who we are *beyond our thoughts and beliefs, it is then we begin to live from the heart.* I would continue to strive to let go of the past, surrender my thoughts, fears, and failures, and to follow my heart into the future.

Chapter 8

Spring Forest Qigong and Covid

I WAS FIRST INTRODUCED TO SPRING FOREST QIGONG RIGHT IN THE middle of all the trauma surrounding my husband's imminent death. It became the one implemented tool in my tool belt of survival skills as I set forth to understand the wherefore and the why of my life in an effort to ease my pain around all that had occurred to date. That one tool would prove indispensable to me in staying the course on the rocky road ahead. I discovered this tool during the winter of my husband's illness shortly after I had the restraining order lifted so that my husband could return to the farm for his last days on earth. He had told his family that he was advised he had approximately three months to live. He had by-passed that prediction by many months already by the time I invited him home.

Things were going relatively well despite my being somewhat debilitated from a recent knee replacement surgery. At one point

I felt that he should be the one taking care of me rather than the reverse, as he continued to enjoy driving around, going to town for coffee with his buddies, and eating three hearty meals a day while I hobbled about with my walker post-surgery. As his condition worsened, he decided to self-medicate with THC along with the CBD oil he had been using. It was probably time for prescribed pain medication like morphine, but he resisted that suggestion as people often do when imagining that would mean their days were numbered. Unfortunately, as had happened in the past whenever Bob used marijuana, he cycled into a manic episode followed quickly by psychosis. As was always the case in the past, he refused to listen to his family's urging to seek help, but a friend was finally able to convince him that he needed psychiatric intervention. He was admitted to the psychiatric unit of the local hospital just days before Christmas.

Needless to say, the holidays were stressful that year. Bob was given a day pass to spend Christmas with his daughter and her family while I stayed home alone. He was consistently playing us one against the other, speaking against me when he was with them, and speaking against them when he was with me. This method of triangulation is just one of the ways that narcissists and controllers manipulate others, especially those closest to them. Other methods he often employed were excessive criticism often veiled as witticism, soliciting sympathy to evoke attention, attempting to isolate me from others, blame shifting and gaslighting, emotional blackmail, etc. I didn't have the strength to care or consider making his manipulations known. It simply didn't matter at this point. I just felt glad to have a few days reprieve from it all.

Once he was in the safety of the psychiatric unit of the local hospital, I followed my instincts and acted spontaneously. I signed up for a week-long Qigong retreat in Mexico. I was desperate to escape all the drama going on in my life, so despite not even knowing what Qigong was or whether or not I might benefit from the experience, I would once again follow my instincts, trusting my gut to steer me right.

I wholly believe the old adage, "When the student is ready the teacher will come." That one week spent learning some of the basics of this particular modality in Traditional Chinese Medicine (TCM) called Spring Forest Qigong (SFQ) would provide a foundation for me to weather the storms ahead in a brand-new way. It would keep me grounded, centered, and calm, despite whatever was going on around me. During the week of that Qigong retreat, something just 'clicked' for me. It was exactly what I needed at the time.

SFQ is a medicinal form of Qigong developed by Master Chinyi Lin, who tells his story in his memoir, *Born A Healer,* and expands upon a clearer understanding of Energy Medicine in, *Head to Toe Healing.* The facilitator of the retreat in Mexico, Sue Crites, didn't spend a lot of time teaching us the philosophy of SFQ. Rather, she simply led us through the meditative movements of the practice for 90 minutes each morning that we were there. We practiced on the beach at sunrise every day. Sue gave us a practical application of Qigong through slow, meditative, repetitive movements, coupled with visualization, conscious intention, and sometimes sound (specific chants for specific movements). We learned that each movement also corresponds to one of the five elements of wood, fire, earth, metal, and water, as well as to the seasons, to our organ systems, and to energy meridians and channels in the body.

When our organ systems honor nature's rhythms, our human systems are brought into alignment with nature. Consequently, the organ systems in our bodies are circling in coherence and integration of mind, body, and spirit.

The purpose behind the practice of medicinal qigong is to bring into coherence all the functions of the physiological self, the mental, emotional self, and the spiritual self, thereby powering up our very own internal resources to help ourselves heal.

Traditional Chinese medicine in itself is founded on the concept of maximizing the functions of the body to remain in health and wellness rather than treating symptomology and disease. TCM is healthcare based on tuning into the internal healing capacities and resources inherent in all of us.

In SFQ we also consciously practice letting go with each exhalation of breath. We release anything that keeps us tethered to the past. We release dysfunctions, diseases, diagnosis, and self-defeating thoughts and emotions. We imagine all of this that no longer serves us leaving our bodies like smoke or butterflies and returning to the universe. This became one of my favorite parts of my Qigong practice as I had a whole helluva lot to be letting go of!

It sounds complicated (and studying in depth may well prove to be so), but the practice itself is so simple you wonder how something so simple could be so effective. Master Lin says, "If you believe it, it works, if you don't believe it, it still works."

Well, it certainly worked for me. It immediately balanced my emotions, calmed my overactive mind, and helped me feel less stressed, moving through my days with much more ease. In the weeks and months to come, I would continue to practice Qigong every single day. As Covid restrictions were put into place preventing people from being in public, the SFQ community offered a 100-day practice on Facebook every day. What a gift this was. I learned so much by following a variety of group leaders, each with their own unique way of incorporating the Qigong techniques into a practice.

I found that no matter what else was going on in my world (and there was a lot going on!), when I did the work to balance the energies flowing through my body, my heart, and my mind, I equipped myself with the ability to move through challenges more quickly. Negative emotions, hurt feelings, and confusion still presented themselves, but when my internal energies were in balance, hard to handle external realities were so much less lingering. I could feel them, acknowledge them, and move through them easily. I was experiencing more mental clarity and a deep underlying sense of well-being. I found this newfound practice so rewarding I would later augment what I had learned on retreat by taking Spring Forest Qigong Level One, Level Two, and a Five Elements Masterclass online. My daily practice of SFQ would become the life raft that carried me through the next year of my life as I traversed all my internal landscapes in an attempt to heal all the ways in which I felt broken.

I returned from the Qigong retreat in Mexico in February of 2019 as the world was just beginning to go into lockdown as a result of the Covid 19 pandemic. So began a strange time of our lives unlike anything we'd ever known before on a global scale. Over the next few years, the world as we had once known it would come crumbling down around us as people strived to survive the restrictions that the pandemic would place upon them and the myriad of losses they were suffering as a result of it. Two short decades into the new millennium people of our planet found themselves facing desperate measures of existence like never before. The circumstances of Covid 19 weren't any worse than the wars, pandemics and natural disasters that had come before in the history of our world, but people were unfamiliar and ill equipped with *how to cope with isolation and the wars raging within themselves.* Forced into isolation, they were having to abandon their outer worlds for their inner landscapes. No one was immune — not even the rich and famous — either to the biological virus that first reared its ugly head upon us or to its aftermath; the loss of familiarity of the world as we once knew it. Like Atlantis, our world was sinking, and people's hearts and souls were being towed under the currents of fear, uncertainty and inevitable change. They struggled to find their footing in an overwhelming state of loss and grief.

Grief, profound in all its forms, prompted us to reevaluate everything. When we were asked to not attend weddings that celebrate love and hope for the dream of happily ever after, or to attend memorials for the loss of the life of a loved one, we were being robbed of the rituals that brought comfort and meaning into our lives.

We asked who we were now, as unemployment escalated and businesses closed their doors. Who were we now, homeless and destitute as real estate went through the roof and available housing dwindled? Who were we now, when stressors accumulated, and relationships strained to the breaking point? Who were we now when corrupt politics and racism ravaged our countries? Who were we now when the world stopped? Meanwhile our hearts kept on beating, our lungs kept on pumping and our blood kept on flowing.

It has been said that the eyes are the mirror of the soul. Masks couldn't hide the broken spirits I could see behind so many eyes. Maybe we were meant to take some symbolism from the fact that when wearing our protective masks, only our eyes remained visible. Maybe it would be our 'vision' that would inevitably be our salvation to a new and better world. Maybe we could envision being really happy. Maybe we could envision abundance. Maybe we could envision peace. If we truly embraced Gandhi's "be the change we want to see in the world," then each of us would venture forth on their own healing journey.

In taking ownership of that responsibility, we could serve humanity better. I believe that we are most closely in tune with our soul when we are living through our hearts, that being centered in our hearts is where we make the connection between our physical selves and our spiritual selves. Regardless of where the future would take us, with spirits broken we became the walking wounded. We would all need to seek support of one kind or another to help us navigate through the grief and the loss we had all suffered. We would all need to venture forth toward some semblance of a healing journey. Whatever a person's issues are, whatever their circumstance, we all need healing in some aspect of our lives. We all feel pain however it might manifest in life.

As many prophets of our times cite, as is on the outside, so it is on the inside. And so, the state of our world inevitably becomes the state of our 'being.' There is a password that Spring Forest Qigong practitioners recite routinely which cites, "I am in the universe, the universe is within me, the universe and I combine together as one." Our external environments largely define our internal landscapes. The internal challenges people faced had never been greater. So, it didn't feel particularly ironic to me that the dark night of *my* soul wasn't too different from what so many other people in the world were going through as a result of the pandemic. I don't remember exactly where I had seen or heard COVID noted as an acronym, but I thought it was a profound one: Concentrate *One's* *V*ision *I*nward *D*ivine

As emotions rose up out of the ashes of our grief, our healing journeys were bound to be tearful ones, wrought with fear and anxiety for the unpredictability of a life gone awry. As we took those first tentative steps back to ourselves, we would inevitably be faced with the dark recesses of our souls own deepest despair. We would question our own validity as we slowly turned from our material world to Spirit. We would shed our old ways to make way for the new as we slowly learned to let go of all that no longer served us. In doing so, we would begin to live our lives on purpose, no longer so bound and directed by society's mores, but with clear intention, and with reverence for the very life we have been blessed to live, despite it all.

Was what was going on for me going on for others? As surely as my wounds became the fertile ground for my healing and my growth, so, too, the aftermath of Covid became the cocoon from which metamorphosis would occur and from which we could all emerge *transformed*. I would find many of my answers in self-sanctuary, where I learned to listen to my heart, and to intuit signs, symbols and messages from spirit. When I was deeply invested and *In To It*, I could begin to *Intuit* how to heal my fractured spirit.

I believe, too, that *the world's trauma will become its medicine.* Astrologers and seers worldwide profess that the world is indeed shifting into a new consciousness, a time of awakening that is predisposed by the apocalyptic nature of world events happening *now.* Apocalypse literally means 'to be revealed.' It's not that things are getting any worse, but that we are more aware than ever before of all that's conspiring on our planet. It seems people are coming to a new awareness or understanding that the old system of doing things, societal patterns and social mores will no longer work to heal the damage done. A new sense of sovereignty is being born — a time of individuals stepping into their (individual) power. When people are pushed into a corner, they will instinctively push back, and that push back looks different now as many more people exercise their right to say no and find the courage to break free by engaging the inner resources they carry within themselves. It is as though we are becoming a generation of healers (the healing generation), and while personal healing illuminates one's life from the inside out, so, too, will it bring a new dimension to social change. The future selves we are birthing will influence the collective. It can't help but do so like the ripples in the water from a single pebble being thrown.

Mental and emotional well-being and health has never been more important. Finally, credence is being given to finding balance between our work and our home lives, to the importance of self-care in working environments where burnout runs rampant. Holistic healing methods have finally even become recognized and invited into the corporate arena, in guise as preventative health measures and self-care practices which are incorporated into the workplace as mental health sessions for employees. Scientific research now recognizes and supports concepts that were once considered to be defined solely by religion or the occult. Logical or linear thinking people take refuge in the scientific fact that we are all biologically wired and have biological responses to life stressors (the fight or flight response, etc.). It has become a more widely accepted notion that everyone benefits from self-regulation and/or relaxation techniques that enhance our ability to think clearly and generate productivity and well-being. So many concepts whose time has finally come are now being talked about and embraced in the mainstream. Eventually, I imagine our mainstream consciousness will look a whole lot different than it has in the past. It is truly the 'Age of Awakening.'

Chapter 9

Crisis to Opportunity/
A Call to Action

TRADITIONAL CHINESE PHILOSOPHY CONSIDERS THAT THE FLIP SIDE of crisis is opportunity, and so it was with the pandemic, for suddenly all manner of educational opportunities were presented to us free of charge via the internet. Where once we had to pay for flights to foreign cities to attend conferences on any manner of training opportunities, here they all were at our disposal. Countless podcasts and webinars on anything and everything were right at our fingertips, most particularly on any manner of holistic healing modalities. Or, maybe the synchronicity of the universe was simply bringing them into my inbox because that was the route *I* had chosen.

Regardless, the internet was to become my classroom, and practitioners of energy work, holistic psychology, psychic mediumship, sacred geometry, dreamwork, sound therapy, numerology, and astrology (and all things woo woo) would become my textbooks.

I would take a seven- week course on supporting those suffering from grief and loss to certify me as a volunteer telephone support worker for a Grief and Loss Society in my local city. I would take advantage of 24 free therapy sessions offered to me as retribution through a Crime Intervention Support program. I would sign up for numerous online Master classes with Mindvalley, Sounds True, and The Shift Network. My studies included classes, workshops, podcasts, webinars, and books.

I had always loved learning in any way shape or form, so I was in my glory having so many opportunities to do so at my own pace, on my own time, and most particularly at no cost, or minimal cost. I filled three journals full of notes on everything that struck me as profoundly relevant and enlightening. I often felt or thought that the teachers and the writers, who I viewed as new age lightworkers, were speaking directly to me and for me, again reiterating that when the student is ready the teacher will come. I felt as though I had a band of angels holding me up and giving me strength and guidance as I traversed my dark night of the soul.

In retrospect, I look back on the winter following my husband's death as the dark night of my soul because the next two years became the most intense period of my entire life. Never before had I ever been so acutely 'aware'! Every thought that came to mind and every feeling I felt was pondered over. My feelings became a roadmap for discovering what was going on for me in my body, and my thoughts were the supporting characters in the play that was the reality of the life I was living. We are the only animal in the animal kingdom that can self-reflect and evolve our consciousness.

Books became a great learning tool for me during this time. After reading Robert Moss,' *The Three Only Things*, I was striving to hone my intuition by examining what was going on for me emotionally. How often have you said to yourself or someone else, "I just had a feeling about it?' and what you meant by that is that you sensed a 'knowing' within yourself that defied rhyme or reason, and just is. My gut instincts / intuitions became more finely tuned the more I used them. This first book of Robert Moss' that found itself into my hands when it fell off the shelf at the second hand bookstore I frequent led me to read more titles written by him. This led me to study 'dreamwork.' What an insightful experience that became! This new direction also came to me at a time when I was having particularly disturbing dreams (more aptly termed nightmares). I began to follow the directions advised, recording my dreams immediately upon awakening (even if in the middle of the night), posing questions, setting intentions or seeking direction prior to sleep. Rarely were the answers or clues blatantly apparent. Yet, the longer I recorded — only to re-read again and again — the more clarity I would gain. One of the approaches given was to not ask, "What does this mean?" but to enquire instead, "What is happening?"

It seemed the moment I set the intention to seek clarity through my dreams the universe threw it at me fast and furious. I don't know if the next three months of turmoil were grief, or relief, but my dreams were fraught with messages of woe and strange disjointed remnants of raw emotion. More often than not in that time period things were resurfacing that I prayed I would never have to live through again. And yet, in dreaming them, it was like I was reliving them.

I recall one disturbing dream I was having about my husband where traumas from my past were resurfacing. Grief has a pace of its own, but I questioned how many times I would have to ponder the circumstances of the past and say goodbye before my pain had spent itself. Sometimes I'd awaken downright angry, and I'd scream aloud, "What the fuck? I've done the fucking work. Leave me the fuck alone!" It seemed that despite forgiveness, compassion and even death, he was still there haunting me, and I was still running for my life. It felt so unfair. I was saying my prayers. I was meditating. I was practicing my energy medicine. I was reading and studying, growing and healing. Yet, there it was.

Dream theorist and Swiss psychologist, Carl Jung, believed that dream divination was an organizing principle in the depths of our soul. So, what was my soul wanting me to know?

Books by Robert Moss reeled me into the landscape of my dreams where answers lay hidden in my subconscious mind. The weird and random people and places that show up when you are deeply asleep can be both strange and fascinating, like a puzzle whose pieces seem to click into place after a time. Keeping a dream journal was one of the most insightful segments of my healing journey when after a day or two of reflection suddenly a newfound clarity could be found.

I recall one dream that must have been so traumatic for me that I couldn't remember it (a self-preservation coping mechanism for sure). All I remembered was that my husband was front and center, the lead actor in the plot. I awoke feeling terribly out of sorts, sort of shaking in my bones, and not really knowing why. One thing did come through for me in that dream — one word. I awoke that morning with one word stamped into my brain and consciousness like a burning brand, and I didn't even know what the word actually meant. But you can be sure I would look it up asap, and I did.

The word was: nefarious. Definition: typically of an action or an activity wicked, evil, or criminal.

I had a deep underlying feeling of my having to trust the truth of it. And I was resistant to doing so as I had spent my whole life practicing denial of this very idea in relation to my husband. Why? Because if his intentions were evil, what did that make me? But on this day, I found acceptance and somehow in shifting to that place of acceptance, my heart was set free from one more tether.

One night I had a confusing dream that I desperately wanted to decipher. In the dream, I was holding a newborn baby high up in the air, laughing up at her as she giggled back at me. I just knew she was a part of my family, so for the next few days I pondered who in the family would be having a baby girl. When the scene in my dream changed that same night, I believed it to be a separate dream altogether. My mother came into a room where I was bleeding on the bed, and she exclaimed, "That's a lot of blood, Char!"

For whatever reason I never connected the two separate scenes of my dreams that night as I have found I can dream many different stories in one night's dream travels. Eventually, however, I came to understand that the baby girl in the dream was me, and I would have to bleed out the pain in order to birth her. Not only would I give birth to a new me, but I would have to re-parent her in all the new ways I now knew how after having learned from the mistakes I made parenting my own children and the mistakes my parents made doing the best they could at the time.

Chapter 10

Learning Tools

ANOTHER BOOK THAT WAS INTEGRAL TO MY HEALING WAS, *The Four Agreements*, by Don Miguel Ruiz. At a time when I was feeling particularly persecuted by my children and others, I would learn how not to take it personally. If somebody said something that triggered me, I learned to accept that whatever was going on for them was theirs, and whatever I was feeling in response to them was mine. Taking ownership for my feelings and inviting the trigger into my conscious awareness allowed me to know myself better. By truly acknowledging this (there it is here and now!), the validation helped to get it unstuck so it could heal. I would practice how not to take other people's comments personally over and over again.

I learned not to make assumptions. Doing so could get me into trouble because I would often act on the assumption I made that was inherently wrong to begin with. I came to understand that I was most apt to make assumptions about things and about other people's behaviors when I was feeling vulnerable, judged, or attacked, and would invariably find a way to place blame. Eliminating the assumption helped me to stop blaming and got me back on course more quickly by not taking it personally.

To be impeccable with your word was an easy one for me as the remnants of Catholicism kept me from ever telling a lie, and a deep abiding quest for integrity kept me mindful of what I was speaking. But, I found that another piece of this pie was following through with one's word. I was pretty good about this. I rarely — if ever — let someone down. If I said I was going to do something, if I said I was going to be there, I did it, and I showed up. But I have experienced the disappointment of people who have let me down in not following through with their word. And I can't help thinking less of them or find that their integrity is diminished in my opinion of them. Not to mention that when someone lets you down, it simply hurts.

Furthermore, to always do one's best was another of the four agreements and a lesson I was hearing from many different sources as I explored all the ways in which I beat myself up about not being good enough. Failure is inevitable, but we need to consider the notion of failure as just one more step in the right direction in learning where not to step next time. In this way, we move from the experience of feeling disempowered to feeling empowered.

Perfectionism is a shame response. Healthy striving is always a better choice. Sometimes we just don't show up in the world as the best version of ourselves, so we need to be able to know ourselves without judgment (and not go to self-blame and shame). We can look at our choices and sometimes say, "What were you thinking?" Then we laugh over the fact that we made the wrong choice that time.

It's the nature of being human, after all, to fuck up sometimes. Be gentle with yourself. You can miss so much if you're afraid of making a mistake. Go ahead and make mistakes. You'll miss less than if you didn't do it, anyway. Simply strive to always do your best, and in doing so, it is, and you are, always good enough!

Another technique (and tool in my toolbox) that has helped me to get stuff unstuck and move through whatever is blocking my progress has been the Emotional Freedom Technique (EFT) of Tapping. Founded by Stanford engineer, Gary Craig, in the 1990's, it is being used worldwide to relieve emotional problems, stress, chronic pain, addictions, phobia, post-traumatic stress disorder, and physical diseases. It has been implemented in classrooms to calm students, by athletes, and by war veterans. Though not endorsed by the American Psychological Association, it is widely used today among a variety of health practitioners and lay people.

EFT is a tool for reprogramming the brain from self-limiting beliefs we assume in childhood or acquire along the way. These beliefs became so much a part of the fabric of our being and so entrenched through all the years we unconsciously lived by them, that later in life they are showing up for us as illness in the body, or emotional despair, or mental health challenges. Before beginning a tapping session, one measures the value of their distress on the SUD (Subjective Units of Distress) scale. Your number will decrease every single time you tap, sometimes significantly, even after only ten minutes of practice. And face it, everybody wants a quick fix these days. Obviously, the problem won't have found its cure the first time around, but like anything else, practice makes perfect, or in my preferred wording, practice makes progress.

I studied EFT online with Nick and Jessica Ortner, did a nine day Tapping challenge with Dawson Church, a masterclass with Teresa Lear Levine, and studied the work of other renowned EFT mentors and practitioners. Like Qigong, the simplicity of Tapping defies its extraordinary effectiveness. Again, like Qigong, it is relatively simple to learn so that you are empowered to do the work by yourself. It is certainly helpful to follow along with guides the first few times, but I love it when I discover, "I can do this!"

The technique lies in expressing what is going on for you while tapping on specific meridian points on your head and your body. When you tap on specific acupressure points, you are sending messages to your amygdala (the stress center of your brain), so you are calming the mind and the body while releasing the core resistance that is keeping us stuck or ill. The root causes or effects are first addressed (you need to prep the ground and pull the weeds and dig and delve before you can nourish the soil). You begin with the experience of whatever is going on for you, move to the thoughts associated with the experience, and then to the emotions that you're feeling around it. In this way, you are firstly validating and acknowledging it, and then declaring that you're not going to succumb to the struggle it brings or fight it any longer. You decide to no longer give it any more power over you, for you're going to surrender it to the universe and welcome in your desired outcome.

The endless little wars we wage within us; the ones in our heads telling us we're not good enough, the ones in our hearts triggering fear or worry, the ones in our bodies showing up as pain and discomfort, can all be an invitation to find some small semblance of peace within ourselves. Because we can! We can move the energy.

With our words and our actions, we move energy and become proactive in our most profound healing ventures. When you change the energy in your body, it doesn't matter anymore what you're thinking or feeling. Your mindset (assumptions and attitudes) has shifted. A deep abiding sense of security overrides it all. You feel stronger. You feel safe. Energy is neither positive nor negative, but neutral. It cannot be changed, but it can be transformed. The practices of Qigong and of EFT can show you how.

Engaging in energy healing practices like Qigong and EFT isn't an overnight fix. Nothing is. What they are is a means by which we can take a vacation from the inherent challenges that being human brings and will continue to bring, no matter what. There are three constants that human beings are faced with. They are: 1) busy minds (monkey mind), 2) chasing unfulfilled desires. and 3) discomfort in our bodies. We all experience discomfort in our bodies, and we generally want to wish it away or run away from it rather than embrace it (even the pain). But mindfulness is to be in our bodies despite the discomfort, and this is what it means to be 'grounded.' When we perceive pain as something we have to defeat or battle against, the energy of focusing on something we don't want (the pain) actually feeds the source of the pain. Knowing the body is a message center for our emotions, we have to make our pain an ally, and talk to it as if it were a friend. Healing the pain happens as the by-product of the higher vibration of love.

Every time you engage in a spiritual practice you transcend those states of discomfort in your body, your monkey mind, and your deepest unfulfilled desires. These are challenges we are one and all faced with and will continue to be faced with throughout our live-long lives. The more time we spend taking a break from these conditions by focusing instead on feeling present and centered in our bodies and focused in our hearts toward something better, the more chances we have of cultivating the elusive dream of happiness and joy that we all seek.

Well-being means to drop into the well of 'being,' which is available to us in every moment. In energy medicine practices, we find the clarity and the discernment to commit to our well-being. Healing is not about fixing the issue or simply healing the pain but about being in peace despite it all. When you have the courage and the persistence to commit to a spiritual practice, often your daily struggles will fall to the background and bring new purpose to the forefront. Eventually, the challenges we all face will no longer pull you under. They will just fall away, and all that shit won't matter anymore because of the strength of spirit residing within you. You will have found the internal source of peace and contentment that you had sought so hard for in the external world.

Chapter 11

Acceptance

I OFTEN FELT FRUSTRATED AND SOMETIMES EVEN ANGRY THAT JUST when I thought I had crossed a major barrier, healed an old wound, or broken an old self-defeating pattern by gaining insight into it, I would often find myself once again reliving the past (betrayal, pain, confusion) all over again. It would resurface time and again, both in dreams and in my waking moments….and it pissed me off! I'd think… this isn't fair! I'm doing the work, I've made so much progress because I'm so much more self-aware than before. What am I doing wrong? If there is a source to this acute pain, what could it be?

I came to understand that this was *exactly* the process by which old patterns and old memories finally get cleared away once and for all. When we are trying to clear up an old issue all the refuse will rise up again and again until it finally gets washed away in the onslaught. Something greater than us is at work for us. All of these broken-hearted moments of remembrance are just another call to action. First, to make peace with the part of you that doesn't like what it's seeing or feeling and to come to full acceptance of what it is and what it isn't. When we achieve self-acceptance, we naturally move toward self-compassion. Then we can understand that the sadness and the pain are essential (the primary motivation) to moving forward.

I had finally learned to listen to my body, to understand when there was something going on that meant it was asking for my attention. So, to live in the darkness another moment was simply to keep on keeping on, that I might eventually find the answer and the light on the other side of it.

My calls to action were sometimes to call on the support of the universe, on God and the angels and all the departed ancestral souls, asking for support and guidance. Sometimes my call to action was to consider that a wound is only ever trapped energy that has gotten trapped in time, and that I could help move that energy with a Qigong practice, with setting an intention, in a meditation, or with the Effective Freedom Technique. I began to get a clear understanding that whatever is going on for you inside (thoughts and emotions) is going to create a condition outside (physicality).

Sometimes my call to action was simply to get the hell out of my own way, and to surrender and trust that everything was going to be okay. Michael Singer, author of *The Untethered Soul* writes a whole second book on this concept alone. Singer explains that the simple act of surrendering (of letting go) can become a most powerful spiritual practice in itself, for it is in the surrender of your will, your concepts and views, and in stepping outside of your mind's constant chatter that you will find your soul center and reside in a state of peace. If you wonder how to get there, he advises practicing on acceptance of the weather.

Acceptance is the bedfellow of surrender for it is that place and moment when you are willing to be in the moment, even if the moment brings discomfort. Surrender is often *letting go of our resistance* to something that's happening. In the absence of resistance, you are in trust. In surrender, you are in trust and in alignment with divine source energy and in co-creation with the universe that holds its destiny in its hands. Our main obstacle is often our unwillingness to experience the withdrawal we must live through when letting go of something. Letting go is to relax, and to release. One of the most difficult (and therefore the most effective) examples of letting go is when we suffer the criticism and judgment of others.

In his anger toward me for going through with divorce, my husband spent many months devising stories with the intent of turning my children against me, and to a great degree. he fully succeeded. I only got snippets of some of what he was professing to be true, but for whatever reason, they believed him at the time, leaving me feeling terribly hurt and abandoned by those very people I loved the most. Letting go of their tarnished opinions of me wasn't easy, but something deep inside of me told me that doing so would be absolutely essential to my healing. And so, I simply surrendered.

To be in defense of your very character is a natural reaction. However, defensiveness is the nature of ego. It didn't take me long to understand that attempting to defend myself would only be a waste of time and energy that I could be using to generate my much-needed peace of mind. So, I could finally see this situation clearly for what it was. It wasn't mine for me to carry, it was his, and it was theirs. I wouldn't take it personally. I could accept it, and I could let it go. I could relax and release it. I used it to motivate me in finding further peace.

Louise Hay says that you can't clean the house if you can't see the dirt. If any dilemma that came my way needed more validation and work, the universe would show me the dirt! And if I didn't listen and ignored the signs, it would shout it out louder and clearer until I did. It would escalate the trouble, or accentuate the problem, or hand me a bigger one. Again, our own resistance to dealing with what's hurting us can become the bigger problem. Dealing with pain isn't about fixing it or finding a solution. The solution is the acceptance of it being the way it is, and being at peace with it, regardless.

We all know the mantra to that one, and it's not wrong.

"It is what it is!"

This place of acceptance is accompanied by an underlying feeling of contentment, and contentment makes room for clarity to surface, for an abiding sense of 'knowing' to take root.

So, I learned to really listen to my instincts, to my feelings, and to my heart. One of my favorite practices, inspired by Lee Harris, is to write in my journal, "What does my soul want me to know today?"

I then take a couple of slow, deep breaths to clear my mind and just allow the words to flow out of me naturally without pause or pressure. My intuition found a voice of its own through this practice, as my soul-self began to speak to me. Intuition isn't logical or intellectual, it is the voice of ourselves as spiritual beings having a human experience. We need to find our own resources to save ourselves. No one else is going to rescue us. The more time you spend looking, the more you will find...answers, solutions, resolve.

Remember, the answers won't be found in our minds wandering, in the incessant narratives of the voices in our heads, for they are simply an expression of our psyche, which isn't at all who we really are. The answers will be found in the sanctuary of the quiet and in the stillness of our hearts and souls, where our true consciousness resides. We are all born of a womb, and it is back to the womb of our soul selves we must return to find our essential power source. Our soul selves reside in that place of peace that is immediately at our disposal...in acceptance and surrender.

The state of our world today is another example of how difficult it can be to let go or surrender to all that's going on around you.

I don't want to accept racism, discrimination, corruption, poverty and violence. But we cannot justify our righteous indignation or anger against it all, for in the expression of our angst we are only contributing to the wrongs by directing our energy there. When we remain in our sole (soul) state of compassion and love, we engage in a purification process that is much farther reaching than simply the state of our own being; we instigate the universe toward purification and peace.

Another route is to seek answers or direction with divination tools such as oracle or tarot cards. There are so many beautiful and inspiring oracle decks available, and every card has a lovely message just for you at that very moment. They can just be fun, lighthearted and frivolous, or seriously relevant and applicable. Renowned oracle card author and reader, Colette Baron Reid, suggests that you treat your cards with reverence by blessing them and clearing them of past energy before each use. She suggests readying yourself for a reading, however brief, by firstly *grounding yourself into a neutral state of mind* with a brief meditation or calming ritual or a simple prayer. She encourages you to *remain curious and open minded*, and to remember that readings are most often more prescriptive than predictive.

In reading oracle cards or using any other kind of divination tool, we need both our analytical and logical minds and our intuition to decipher the messages they hold for us. Collette believes that the most important card of your reading is the first card you select, which is your anchor card, or the foundation card for the rest of the reading. Your second rule is to *let go* of your attachment to any desired outcome, allowing spirit to give you guidance and direction. When you want what you want but can't see past your attachment to that particular outcome, you may not be open to hearing the rest, or you may miss the gist of the message altogether.

A one card reading can be wholly insightful. It often denotes where you are now. A second card is often seen as denoting where you are heading, while a third card might further show what the potential outcome will be. A fourth card is often chosen when the message is unclear, and you want further clarity. More often than not, the cards you pick are generally simply a reflection of the answers you already have within you, but it's so nice to have it spelled out for you much more definitively in beautiful language and art.

One day, I asked myself how I could feel such peaceful contentment in my heart and mind, and yet find my body wracked with pain. Obviously, arthritis is painful at times, but in believing there's an emotional foundation to physiological pain, I would seek to find it on any given day of acute pain. So, one day I picked an oracle card from my Rumi deck, authored by Alana Fairchild, posing the question of what the source of my pain could be.

I never choose a card, but rather, I shuffle and shuffle until one literally falls out of the deck on its own. One always does. The card that fell out in front of me that day was titled "Divine Discontent," and it spoke loudly and clearly to my question. It read, "Don't misinterpret the pain and think something is wrong. Its purpose is to lead you into your greatest connection yet, to divinity." And Rumi asks that my prayer on this day be just this: "I surrender. I surrender in sacred trust."

Oh, how desperately I needed to hear that message on that day. I needed to recognize my fear of inhabiting a broken body that I have been unable to heal despite all my concentrated efforts.

I now understand that my peace of mind and my heart's contentment will grow even stronger the more I surrender the destiny of my days to the divine. And I need to remember and affirm that I am not broken. I am whole. And that I can love and accept myself just the way I am.

Chapter 12

Self Care and Boundaries

ONE OF THE FIRST LESSONS I LEARNED ALONG MY WAY WAS THAT it is essential to tend to your self-care when you're feeling depleted or defeated by life. Essential self-care is absolutely non-negotiable. Self-discovery work and transformational healing can be emotionally exhausting. It is both terrifying and exhilarating. Emotional exhaustion in itself can be terribly debilitating and more difficult to diagnose if you have never learned what it means to take care of yourself. It sounds ridiculous to not inadvertently attend to nourishing your body and self-grooming, but true self-care looks like much more than that. And for many, especially those prone to codependent behaviors like I was — accustomed to putting others' needs ahead of my own — taking deeper, more meaningful care of myself was a foreign concept.

Oprah calls it the disease to please. Self-Love? What the hell even is that? There was irony in feeling like a strong, confident woman who really liked herself, but not knowing how to love myself. Loving yourself must override anything anyone else has ever done to you or said to you that hurt. You need to become your own best friend, your own best medicine, your own hero, your very own knight in shining armor, remembering that *only you can rescue you.*

I literally had to write the words, "I love you," on the bathroom mirror to remind myself to say the words in hopes that the affirmation that felt like a pretense would one day become true for me. And it did. But, not without concentrated efforts. I was well-practiced at survival and self-preservation, but I really didn't understand the notion of loving oneself, so I would need to explore what it really meant, and moreover, what it might look like in practice.

The biggest aspect of self-love that I *first* needed to learn was about *boundaries;* learning to set them for myself and learning to respect the boundaries of others. Here was another concept I really didn't understand. It was my children who first taught me what boundaries meant, why they were so important, and how honoring them nurtured a high level of regard and mutual respect, not only in our relationships with others but in our relationship with ourselves.

The lack of boundaries and the need to try to control outcomes are two of the quintessential parts of the fiercely codependent personality. A controlling personality is born from deep anxiety that is developed when one's needs aren't met in childhood. The child develops an obsessive coping style. What is originally a desperate response to emotional deprivation becomes controlling behavior — ultimately a pattern of behavior developed to ensure survival. Though I was most definitely this person, I simply didn't recognize myself as being controlling, at all.

I was under the false impression that if I did something with the good intention of trying to help, it was okay to overstep the boundary of it not being any of my business. It became second nature to put my two cents worth into where it didn't belong. When my children would reprimand me for overstepping, however subtly I did so, I would quickly defend myself by proclaiming, "But I was only trying to help," which seemed reasonable to me. It was as though I expected that my good intention would override the inappropriate behavior and make my actions acceptable on that basis. It didn't. I had to own up to the responsibility that what I did in trying to help fix someone else's problem remained unacceptable. It didn't preclude that I was indeed trying to control some outcome that wasn't mine to do. And I would invariably walk away feeling deeply hurt.

Through concentrated effort in examining my feelings, I realized that when I'm feeling hurt (however inconsequential the circumstance) I feel hurt in a BIG way. I immediately go back to remember all the other times I felt hurt by something that person did or said, and I pile all the memories on top of the present circumstance until I've erected a great big wall of shame and regret. And then, in my attempt to knock that wall down, I place an equal amount of fault or blame on the other person. I would then try to outweigh my wrong doing by bringing up all the circumstances when I was doing right, all the times I helped in a good way, imagining, "Don't all those times I really did help cancel out this one time I overstepped?" Nope, it doesn't work that way. Sound convoluted? Hell yeah, talk about making mountains out of molehills!

How could I ensure that once I was able to see it clearly, I could change my behavior next time around? I asked what I would need to tell myself next time around so I wouldn't let it happen again. I figured out that if I was hurt by what felt to me like a rejection of me, just because I feel rejected doesn't mean it's true. Just because they're mad at me in that moment doesn't mean they don't love me.

This is what a trigger looks like. When the present circumstance triggers the memory of feeling that way before and prompts you to react in a bigger way than the occasion calls for. Feeling rejected or judged for doing something that I didn't perceive as being wrong triggered the memory of rarely ever feeling good enough, or worthy of consideration and love. It triggered feelings of inadequacy, of not being heard or seen. All that? Yep.

If I craved admiration and respect (probably mostly because I never got any from my significant other over the past 40 years), well then I had to learn to admire and respect myself enough so as not to be so desperately needing other people's validation and approval. Learning to deal with my emotions by examining them and doing something, or thinking something to help me feel better, became a big step in my self-care handbook. But my big lesson was learning that crossing boundaries is simply inconsiderate and disrespectful. So ultimately, I had to become more aware of my long-held instincts to do things the way I always did them, and become more aware of the times when I might overstep my involvement, and — eager to help or not — just don't fucking do it! I had to stop wanting to rescue and learn to detach. It's important to note, however, that I didn't realize any of this until I took the time to question, "What am I feeling? Why am I feeling this way?" And, "What is really going on for me right now?"

I use this example of boundaries to exemplify the importance of taking responsibility for one's behaviors and ultimately for one's life. Taking responsibility does not mean that one is at fault when problems arise, nor is it about placing blame. Fault resides in past tense and results from choices that have already been made, while responsibility resides in the present and results from choices you're currently making or are about to make.

In taking responsibility, you always have the chance to make a new choice, to choose how you see things, how you react to things, and how you value things. *You choose the metric by which you measure your experience.* People can certainly be to blame for doing something that hurts you, but they are never responsible for how you feel.

When I made the mistake of getting involved in my children's problems by trying to help, but failing terribly by not respecting their boundaries, I craved feeling respected by them, and by others in general, but I first needed to learn how to act in ways that assured others they were respected *by me*.

We absolutely need to do the work it takes to break old patterns of behavior that bring disharmony to our relationships. Doing the work means taking responsibility and honoring boundaries. It sounds like putting up boundaries separate us as we each stand in our own court with fences intact, but ultimately boundaries do exactly the opposite. Boundaries are a way to bring people closer together and to enhance intimacy. For, intimacy is not about sex, but about being real, respectful, vulnerable, loving, and supportive. Platonic relationships can be deeply intimate…if we respect one another's boundaries.

I also had to learn to weave boundaries into my self-care by learning to say no. Saying no meant learning to love myself. The ability to say no is a self-care practice in itself. Where we imagine someone will judge us as being selfish, we learn instead that they will respect our clear messages. Learning to say no was one of the most difficult things I have ever done because always saying yes is a deeply entrenched codependent behavior. I simply didn't know how to make my needs as important as someone else's, especially if I loved them. I'm still practicing.

Incorporating practices to self-soothe, such as taking time for a long candlelight bath or a quiet half hour to myself for a cup of tea, meant learning to love myself. Self-soothing can be as simple as using your breath to center yourself in a place of sanctuary, reaffirming 'I am safe.' I can let it go (the fear, the worry, the anxiety) with gentle deep breaths, and respond in calm. In fear my energies are constricted; in refuge and safety I become open and receptive to healing.

I can show myself all the love and support I need and find my inner resources of calmness and peace, of refuge. I can find my center. I can connect with pure source energy and healing light from above, feel it seeping down through the crown of my head, down through my body and into the core of mother earth, who holds me in the comfort of her womb. She knows me, as she loves me. And her grounded yin energy helps me to process, and to let go.

When I can feel both rooted to the earth and connected to the light of the universe, my energies are aligned, and I am centered. In this space, I am safe and protected. In this space, I find my sanctuary, and my home. Stopping to become aware of your breath and taking a few minutes to imagine yourself filling with healing light and rooting yourself to the earth can be as effective as a lengthy guided meditation. We do indeed have the support of heaven and earth, and it is in this sacred space that you create within yourself that you can more easily reframe your old habitual thought processes and self-defeating beliefs. Here, you can *release* with *real ease.*

There is no such thing as, 'I don't have time to imagine something better for myself, or to take care of myself and *love myself.*' We make all the choices that put us in our present set of circumstances, so *we have to make different choices, and make time for what's important.* Self-care and self-love is *so* important. But we mustn't confuse self-love with self-esteem. Self-esteem is conditional upon achievement. We feel good about ourselves as a reward for a job well done, whereas self-love is *unconditional* love and acceptance. You don't need to earn it; you already deserve it.

You will know when you are making self-betraying choices because you will feel drained, depleted, or a little lost. You are always on the right path, and the universe will give you clues along the way. When a particular segment of the journey feels confusing, you're just not managing the journey that well. You've gotten sidetracked and taken a detour, but there are lessons to be learned every step of the way, and you can always find your way back to the right route, with new choices.

Chapter 13

Reprogram, Affirm, and Envision

ANOTHER MAJOR SEGMENT OF THE JOURNEY WAS TO LEARN HOW to reprogram my mind of my long-held, self-defeating or limiting beliefs (most of them formed from birth to seven years of age) that followed me into adulthood and kept me stuck in expectations of abandonment, scarcity, and unworthiness. As Henry Ford said, "If you think you can, or you think you can't, you're right." And Oprah Winfrey said it well with her statement, "You don't manifest what you want, you manifest what you believe." This work takes considerable time. It is work that can undoubtedly be done with a therapist, but it is possible to do it on your own if you have a willingness to do it and are prepared to put in the time. Ultimately, we are all in recovery: from addiction, from our traumas and from our self-sabotaging behaviors.

Maturation is the process of evolving and of knowing we can outgrow the state of our past (the emotional imprints that are deeply embedded in our psyche) that are still running our present. To do so we will need to be aware that you are likely to come up against some fundamental blind spots (illusions that we cling to). The most prevalent is the belief that if you change the parameters of your circumstance (the partner, the house, the body), the problem will get fixed, and you'll have a different experience. But Gabor Maté professes that if we truly crave change and growth, we don't need to change our lifestyles but to address our childhood wounding, and in doing so the behavioral changes will automatically follow.

When our stringent beliefs take decades to implant themselves into our brains (and then to manifest in self-sabotaging behaviors), we aren't going to shift them overnight. Furthermore, it is said that our ancestral karma finds us born with assignments specific to our individual evolution, and these assignments are the lessons we must learn to clear our karma in this lifetime. This is why we often fall into the same choices and behavioral patterns that defeat us time and again. Because we *are unaware* of *them* because they reside in *our subconscious mind*. And unfortunately the highest percentage of our subconscious thoughts and beliefs are negative, limiting, and disempowering ones. So, our first order of business is to *deprogram* our subconscious, self-defeating thoughts and beliefs and then, and only then, *reprogram* it. Breaking the habit of the old self has to happen before the new self can emerge. Like fixing an engine problem in a vehicle, we need to remove the old worn-out part and install a brand new one. In order to do that, we need the tools to get the job done.

The deprogramming can only happen at a conscious level, so we need to become super vigilant about self-reflection, doing the self-exploratory work of finding out what those beliefs are and where they are showing up in self-sabotaging ways. Otherwise, they will literally stop us in our tracks, and prevent us from achieving all that we desire (to heal, to flourish, to manifest abundance, to nurture contentment, happiness, and peace). In doing so, we are uncovering the subconscious data and bringing it into our conscious awareness. We need to become the constant observer for a while, taking note of how we're responding at every turn. Once we have achieved the awareness of the particular self-sabotaging thoughts or behaviors that show up in any given situation, only then can we change it. And then we need to do it over and over and over again because there will be a number of different ones that need to be discovered, uncovered, and combatted. It seems self-evident, but because we live so much of our lives on automatic pilot (allowing our subconscious programs to lead and direct us through life), it really isn't self-evident at all, until we make it so. Ninety five percent of who we are is our memorized behaviors, hardwired attitudes and perceptions, and automatic emotional responses that have been directing our lives from the inside out like a computer program.

We literally have to spend time every single day reviewing what we are thinking, feeling and intending, (watch how we speak, observe how we act, and pay attention to what we're feeling). We need to become radically honest here and accept that 'here' is where we are, and who we are now in this moment. From that very moment of clarity and refined self-awareness we can begin the process of change or growth. First, we review what we don't want, then we rehearse what we do want. Review and rehearse, review and rehearse.

Relationships are the most revealing place to discover our subconscious programs. The self-defeating program is wherever we're struggling. The learning process comes from making the mistake, or remembering the mistake, and then telling yourself you will do it differently next time. And then doing it differently, over and over again. This is the tool of habituation. Now we are on the right path to deprograming, we are slowly but surely getting beyond our mind and our bodies old habituations, and beginning to rewire our brain, make new choices, and create positive change. The moment of change happens when we are able to remain in conscious awareness. The pursuit of this very concept is the gist of many holistic healing practices (breathwork, meditation, energy work).

The reprogramming work isn't easy, but it is essential to real and lasting change in our lives. You can do this work under the tutelage of Dr. Joe Dispenza in his numerous workshops and seminars, or at Mindvalley with Vishen Lakhiani, who teaches the Silva Mind Control Method, and probably on countless other programs available to us. But you truly can do the work yourself if you have the wherewithal to do so, and the 'sticktoitiveness!' There are no negative side effects of the practice of thinking in a different way. It is the overcoming process that becomes the new becoming process. When we manage and regulate our inner world, our outer world will slowly but surely change to reflect the state of our new inner world. You can't believe in a new future for yourself without first *believing in yourself*, and in your own medicine.

So, where do we find the tools to get the job done? We cultivate them within ourselves. *Habituation* is one tool. Practice and repeat (as you did when you learned to drive a car). Now you drive with your subconscious mind while your conscious mind carries on a conversation with your passenger or is grooving to your favorite tunes. *Hypnosis* is another. A form of self-hypnosis can be achieved when our minds are in a state of Theta. When we awaken our minds move from Delta to Theta to Alpha to Beta. When we are retiring for the night, we move from Beta to Alpha to Theta to Delta. So, we can record positive programing and subliminal messaging and listen to it just before bed or immediately upon awakening. And…we can cultivate being centered and grounded in the present moment (in conscious awareness) with those same holistic healing practices mentioned throughout (energy medicine practices, spiritual practices, meditation, breathwork, yoga, etc). In doing these practices, you are trading the stresses of the old negative beliefs and patterns for the positivity of the elevated emotional state you experience in heart coherence. Your brain then begins to synchronize into coherence or order. It is now being termed heart/brain coherence, and it is the door between the conscious and the subconscious, when you are transported to a hypersensitive learning mode, a place where creativity is prevalent, and serenity abides.

When we engage in all of these practices, we are literally shifting the energy in our bodies from stress mode (which we unconsciously live in most of the time), to the higher vibration of living through our hearts (which happens automatically when we relax). So, if we're practicing relaxation techniques, we are training ourselves in heart/brain coherence. Positive physiological responses happen in this mode. When we are in the relaxed state of heart coherence, it has been documented that there is a spike in immune system functioning. And when we engage in practices that put us into the high vibration of living with an open heart, our mindful intentions are being given an energy boost. Regulating our brain waves is not enough. Intention is not enough. The elevated emotion of heart coherence needs to accompany this beautiful and worthy work.

If you commit to affirming the new beliefs that you want to embody and you affirm over and over and over again, that new belief will indeed take hold, and the circumstances of your life will begin to change to support your new belief.

How do you affirm the new belief? With positive affirmations spoken aloud by saying the words. Whisper them, shout them, write them, read them…I am enough, I am deserving, I am worthy, I am loved…. or any affirmation you have devised on your own by first identifying the negative thought or belief you are fostering. You identify your feelings, and your beliefs, you name them and acknowledge them, allow yourself to give them credence by feeling them, and then you are able to move through them. Shifting them happens with pure intention and so using positive affirmations helps to make the shift happen.

You must formulate your affirmations as though they are already a reality, as though they are already true. It's not *I want to be cherished,* but *I am cherished.* The power of our vocabulary, both our self-talk and our shared talk frames the experiences we have, and the experiences we want to have.

Vishen Lakaihani, in his book, *The Buddha and the Badass,* suggests posing what he calls 'lofty questions' as an alternative to formulating affirmations. Lofty questions may read as follows:

> *Why am I in such a perfect state of health? Why do I have such powerful intuition? Why am I so clear of my goals and visions? Why do all my dreams come true? Why am I such a powerful manifestor? Why is my life so abundant? Why am I always so surrounded by love? Why do I feel so joyous and at peace with my world?*

Can you see how posing these questions opens the door to the universe giving credence to the manifestation of them in your life? Ultimately, you need to find the approach or the tools that most resonate for you. Again, *when the student is ready, the teacher will come.* Are you ready?

Everything we say and do is being recorded by the universe. It's why Karma exists. The sum of a person's actions in this and previous incarnations will help determine their future experiences in life. I believe this to be true, and if it is, I want to live my life in heart/brain coherence, guided by kindness and compassion, and dedicated to making the world a better place...even just by cleaning up my own act!

Perfecting the skill of self-love is so important to your personal growth process, and something as simple as writing *I love you* on your bathroom mirror is a good place to start. Or elaborate.

I love, accept, and honor myself just the way I am.

If you can get over your initial embarrassment over imagining someone might catch you at it, you're on your way. Having the words in places where they are easily noticed and obvious reminders will help you remember and keep you on task. I used to tell my clients to say their daily or weekly affirmations every time they took a pee, when they brushed their teeth morning and night, when they started their car, etc. Doing something over and over again simply works. It's how we learn to play an instrument. My favorite example of this would be when I decided I could teach my father to say I love you. He had left when I was 11 and never returned, and I had never heard those words come out of his mouth. But later in life my family moved closer to where he lived, and we began to talk on the phone on a regular basis. Every time we talked just before hanging up I would say, "I love you dad."

He never said it back. He just didn't know how. It was probably a foreign language to him. But I persisted. Over three years I persisted, when all of a sudden right out of the blue, one day he replied, "I love you too sweetie."

If you want to learn something, repetition works. It is the same rote learning we used when we memorized our times tables in elementary school.

You can't outrun negative thinking, and you don't have to believe your new positive thought the first time you think it. Simply declare it and keep running towards trying to believe it. You must be relentless and determined and give yourself 100 chances to get it right. There is an Aramaic word, "Abracadabra," which translates as "I create as was spoken." And haven't we always associated the word Abracadabra with magic? Of course, we have. Affirmations *are* pure magic. Affirmations are magical mantras that bring about the change we want.

Visualization is the accompanying tool to affirming. I love the play of words, the hidden relevance in their make -up. Consider 'imagine.' Within it we find 'magi.' There is magic in our imaginings, in our visualizations. Just as an electroencephalogram measures brainwaves, so, too, do our visualizations carry electrical charges that show up in our body as biological responses. Angry or aggressive thoughts, or frightening images like man-eating spiders or vampires generate adrenaline in our bodies, while calming, relaxing scenes show up as a tranquilizer, similar to valium or Ativan. If you conjure images of triumph, like a knight in shining armor rescuing the fair maiden in distress, or winning the trophy, you are mobilizing neuropeptides that boost your immune system. Our bodies can't distinguish between an imagined event and a physical event; they both shift the body's electrochemical systems.

The power of healing images being used by patients to help heal their symptoms is now recognized in the medical community as a significant and positive development. The power of our own ability to visualize something better for ourselves is a major key to combating the self-defeating and self-limiting beliefs that keep us stuck in our present set of circumstances. We create the environment that calls healing and miracles to us by raising our vibrations and being in the flow of positivity and of universal love. Consider John Lennon's beautiful song, *Imagine*, and invite all manner of wondrous possibilities into your life by *imagining* how beautiful it could really be!

An effective approach to the visioning process can be to shift how you pose a question to yourself and the universe. Instead of envisioning what it is you have to do to get to your desired outcome, instead envision having already arrived there. So, you end up asking not, "What *do* I *have to do* to get there?" Instead, because you are imagining how wonderful it feels having arrived, having the dream come true, or the miracle realized, you ask "What *did I* do to get here?"

You have all the answers you will ever need right there inside of you. Just ask the questions and listen for the answers. Shhhh, be quiet, be still... and listen.

Ultimately, a constantly growing sense of self awareness and finding new insights into yourself is the first step toward doing the hard work of making changes. In soul searching, we find the answers. So many of the mishaps we encounter are because we simply don't know any better, but once we gain insight into ourselves (our habits and our patterns of behavior), we can make better choices. When we know better, we can do better.

In the end, it is the soul that has shed some light onto the person who inhabits the body, that brings us home to ourselves. It is often called shadow work, because when we're looking at ourselves through all of the lenses of imperfection and all manner of dysfunction that is showing up in our relationships and our life circumstances or in our state of health, we desperately want to be better, to do better, and to grow. The shadow is somewhat out of our field of awareness, and it can truly be a time of deep sorrow, of fumbling our way through the darkness that is our trauma. But when you are riding out the storm or suffering the calamity all over again and fear and uncertainty settles in, don't run from it, walk toward it!

As I said before, we have first to see the dirt — or feel the pain, or get the frightening diagnosis — before we can find a way to sweep it away or to heal it. Facing all of that isn't easy. Remaining in the reality of the emotions is essential to moving forward when the time is right. Pain and discomfort is always a catalyst for change. We need to remember, *to know*, that a time of crisis almost always precludes a time of expansion and transformation. Tears are transcendent. Pain is transcendent. Grief is transcendent. Trust that the discomfort of doing the shadow work will pass. Trust that you will overcome and ascend. Success is born out of the chaos, *born of the shadow work*, with faith in oneself, in determining a future no longer based on the past but of a new future *envisioned*.

We need to develop clarity of vision. We need to paint pictures of a better future for ourselves. We need to shift from remembering the past and its accompanying events, emotions associated with those events, and the beliefs that support them to a kind of remembrance of the future. The familiarity of the past is what keeps us stuck there in our minds, because there is comfort in familiarity, and discomfort in change. In remembering the past and remaining stuck in the familiarity of the event and in the emotion of that event, we give it power and strength, despite wishing it hadn't happened. We tend to hold on to our tragic memories and fall back into what feels familiar, because familiarity just feels right. So, we need to have the awareness of when that happens for us and respond differently by saying, "No, this isn't right, it's just familiar." We need to spend as much time painting the pictures of our futures as we once spent reliving all that came before when we continue to think about it, over and over again. We kind of get stuck in the spin cycle.

We literally need to replace our old stories by writing new ones, envisioning what that new story will look like. Look to the horizon of tomorrow, imagine yourself in that new place, in that new circumstance, how it looks, how it smells, how it feels. Imagine how you look, the expression on your face, the clothes on your back. The more definitive the picture the stronger the vision, the more power it has to come true. Dream big. Bigger than you want to believe possible and envision it clearly! Visionaries are people who strive for a higher ideal. Become your own best visionary for the person you want to be and the new life you want to live.

You have to take the time to do all of this, to install new circuits in your brain. You need to build a whole new conscious awareness of all your old self-defeating emotions and patterns of behavior. And, *memorize new ones on the canvas of your newly envisioned dreamscape.* Clarity of vision is both a mind set and a skill set. Creating vision boards is a fun and easy way to begin. Ultimately, you want to hold the pictures in your mind. It is there where they must become as deeply embedded as your old stories once were in order for you to achieve your goal.

Chapter 14

Goal Setting and Energy Medicine

GOAL SETTING IS ANOTHER IMPORTANT TOOL FOR CHANGE, BUT it's equally important to have a plan of action to support our goals. A plan of action is the only way we can make ourselves accountable and measure our failures and successes. Failures are only one more step toward success. Failure is not followed by an exclamation mark like we are prone to do, but by a comma, and we must keep on keeping on. Goals must be both measurable and achievable in order to be met. Plans of action do just that.

When you want to make a change and don't know where to begin, ask yourself, "What can I do differently? What can I stop doing? What can I start doing?" Then, when you've named the action you are going to take, ask yourself, "When?"

Depending on the action, your answer may be something like, *I will work on my resume Tuesday before noon,* or, *I will go for a fifteen minute walk every Monday, Wednesday and Friday at 7:30 AM.*

Beyond the practical application of action plans is the importance of attaching an emotion or a feeling to the outcomes you desire when you're daydreaming about what you want, and then actually making efforts to detach from what you imagine the outcome to be. This can appear confusing or contradictory, but it's simple, really. If you want to be as specific as 'I want to lose 20 pounds,' attach the emotions you will have when you are feeling so beautifully fit, so strong and healthy, and you will much more likely reach that goal with less effort than if you are just holding yourself to the weight loss goal. Now, herein lies the detachment aspect. If you set the goal of wanting to lose twenty pounds, you are confining the dream to that one narrow outcome, whereas if your goal is to feel beautifully fit, strong and healthy, the universe may well show you how to do that in a myriad of ways other than just by dropping the pounds. Remember, you can lose 20 pounds rather easily and *not* be strong, fit or healthy! You can lose twenty pounds rather quickly when you have a terminal cancer diagnosis. Got it? Yep, you got it.

One of the best scenarios I can share to bring home the notion of attaching a feeling to the desire is to tell you about my first experience on a seniors' dating site at 67 years of age. Talk about a daunting endeavor! I learned so many things about myself on that little jaunt into cyberspace. So, I set the intention to welcome new love into my life. The very moment a man who I was attracted to showed interest in me, I immediately went into negative self-talk mode…he's so good looking, and I'm not young enough, or pretty enough, or smart enough (I can't dance Salsa, and I can't speak Spanish, while he can speak *my* language). Learning to speak Spanish and dance Salsa were things I wanted to learn, but I wasn't good enough… yet. Luckily, I caught myself speaking to myself in these self-doubting ways before our second date and affirmed that I was most certainly worthy of his attention. I immersed myself in feeling worthy, self-confident, and even kind of pretty (wrinkles et al intact), and it worked to spark his further interest in me. He even expressed that he was falling in love with me (after our third date no less!). Wasn't this what I wanted?

What I had failed to do was to attach how I wanted to feel when new love came into my life. Certainly, the bottom line was that I wanted to feel loved. Check. He certainly made me feel admired and gave me back a confidence in myself as a woman that I hadn't felt in a very long time. Yep, he made me feel loved. But, I also wanted to trust him implicitly. I wanted to trust his word, and to trust in his devotion to me. What happened next? He told a small white lie, but it was enough to make me question how much of the person he showed the world was real, and how much a facade. And though I felt equally as drawn to him as he expressed he was to me, I wanted to take a step back and take it slow. He immediately went into the victim role as though I was abandoning him, which absolutely blew me away. I was shocked that he didn't seem to want to continue seeing me if we were to take it slow. Whoa! No devotion there, and ultimately little to put my trust in. So, another lesson learned.

Now, in welcoming new love into my life, I will also welcome not only feeling loved but feeling a deep sense of trust and devotion and much more than that, now that I've learned how to dream big! Was setting the intention to welcome romantic love into my life a goal? In the beginning it probably was, but as time goes on I am much more engaged in the process of *detaching* from the specific outcome of having a man in my life, and *attaching* to the feeling of being cherished for not only who I am as a woman, but for who I am in my heart and my mind and my soul. I want to be loved by someone who really gets me and loves me, anyway.

So, goal setting and supporting my goals with plans of action have become second nature to me, as have various modalities of energy medicine. Beyond my daily practice of Qigugong, one of my favorite energy medicines is tapping of EFT, which was introduced in Chapter Seven. Tapping brings to mind the phrases we often use when we're talking about accessing something important. We say, "Tap into your intuition," Or, "Tap into your memories."

I think about all the tapping we do on our phones and computers to access information. Tap, tap, tap. We even tap, tap, tap on a door for it to be opened. I enjoy the symbolism that is there to be found if we look for it. Tapping exercises don't take a lot of time out of all the other obligations you must fulfill on any given day but like with anything else we do to achieve a desired outcome, we must dedicate ourselves to doing them. Tapping is simply one modality of energy medicine available to us right at our fingertips — pun intended.

Beyond the ones I have mentioned because they were right for me, there are numerous other modalities of energy medicine from which to choose. Reiki or Bodytalk practitioners can do the work for you (as can a therapist in the field of psychology), but I'm devoted to practices that are *self-empowering* in their capacity to heal. Qigong (Qi, meaning life force energy or vitality, gong meaning to work or cultivate,) is one of them. We have sovereignty over our energetic field and can support the flow of energy throughout the energy channels of our body to remove blockages and create harmony.

We are each and every one of us a field of electromagnetic frequency, and we carry these frequencies out into the world, constantly adding to the flow of life simply by living and breathing. When our energies are flowing unencumbered, flowing freely in collaboration with the pure source energy of universal love and light, *we become catalysts for goodness and love*. We *become* the change we want to see in the world.

Acquire whatever tools you like and the practices that resonate for you. The better equipped your tool belt, the better you will fare. Whatever tools or holistic healing modality you might choose to augment your healing journey, you must be committed to being consistent with your practices. Consistency and commitment force us to take the work seriously. It is said that it takes 21 days to form a new habit, and 90 days to make it work, and for true transformation to occur. But I believe that there are some practices that are meant to be never ending if we want to continue to *love our lives* and *remain in our bliss.* The practice of *Gratitude* absolutely fits into this category.

Chapter 15

Gratitude and Forgiveness

PRACTICING GRATITUDE, AND ASSUMING AN ATTITUDE OF gratitude every day, allows you to focus on the bigger picture of how good life is. Being grateful for all that will come your way in the future allows you to see not only all that you will manifest in future but all the wonderful things you have already manifested in your life. Gratitude actually reduces the stress hormone cortisol and increases serotonin in your brain! You mustn't wait for your wealth to feel abundant, or your success to feel empowered, or your healing to feel whole, or a new relationship to feel loved. In an interview with Sonia Ricotti in her Unsinkable Self-Help and Personal Growth program, renowned author, Dr. Joe Dispenza proclaims: "The moment you start feeling worthy and abundant you start generating wealth. The moment you are grateful and start feeling whole your healing begins. The moment you are in love with yourself and your life you will create an equal. The moment you start feeling empowered you step toward success."

In Spring Forest Qigong, the fifth movement in the five-element series of movements is connecting with your heart through "Gratitude." This movement aligns with the kidney system which includes not only your kidneys but your reproductive organs, breasts, hormones, bladder, bones and bone marrow. It also corresponds with the season of winter, with the element of water, and with the color blue, dispelling the negative emotion of fear. So many of our negative emotions are borne of fear that practicing this movement allows you to cover a lot of bases. It's one of my favorite things to do at the start of each day. Many of the psychic weights we carry by staying stuck in negative influences are lifted when we express how thankful we are. Master Chinyi Lin of Spring Forest Qigong says, "You've already won the lottery just by being alive." Be grateful. Everyday.

However, you obviously don't have to do qigong to practice gratitude. Every time I find a parking spot, I say thank you. Every time I sip some water, I say thank you. I say thank you when I'm walking, as I know what it feels like to be debilitated in that regard. I say thank you when I'm cooking because I remember what it felt like to have empty cupboards. I say thank you when I find myself feeling comfortable and warm on a chilly winter morning. And when I run into the water at the lake on a scorching hot summer day. I even say thank you when I look into the mirror — despite that I don't like seeing the wrinkles and the sagging skin on my aged face. I am really and truly so grateful just to be alive.

The practice of *Forgiveness* is also a practice that is essential to your healing. When you are in the resentment of the things you are struggling to forgive, you must truly embrace it first, or it will continue to be re-sent (the root of re-sent-ment). Forgiveness does not mean condoning the wrongdoing, or even reconciling the relationship. You can still forgive even while in no way believing that their actions were acceptable or justified. Acknowledge your anger and your pain. I am angry. I am hurt. I am afraid of being hurt again.

If you don't acknowledge the feelings or take responsibility for them, you won't be able to move to forgiveness. The process is essential to the outcome.

Forgiveness is not so much for the benefit of the other person, but for your own benefit. Forgiveness is the decision to overcome pain that was inflicted by another person. It is letting go of anger, resentment, shame and other emotions associated with injustice. It is treating our offenders with compassion even though they don't deserve it.

Sometimes we want something from someone else that we need to give ourselves, for there is nothing we want from others that we cannot give ourselves. Moreover, we must forgive ourselves for all the choices we made that brought us where we are today, for all the high standards we weren't able to meet, and we beat ourselves up over. We can't embrace our own inherent worthiness if we can't learn to forgive ourselves.

When we are exploring and exposing ourselves to our psychic wounds (some of them simply our areas of vulnerability) in order to know ourselves better, we will invariably uncover mistakes we made along the way, our self-inflicted wounds. In making amends with yourself, you give yourself permission to release all the burdens of self-judgment you carry. Only then can you find the ability to forgive others. Others don't even need to be present, nor even alive for you to forgive them.

Forgiveness is such a high vibrational energy that it dispels anything coming toward it that doesn't align with its compassionate and loving nature. Forgiveness is therefore one of the highest forms of self-protection of your own energy field. The more sensitive and empathic we are toward other people's moods and energies, the more we need to protect ourselves from taking on too much by carrying their pain and suffering or absorbing their sadness or anger.

When I was told by a Body Talk practitioner that I was a strong Empath, she suggested I needed to be aware of my propensity to do this, and to protect myself. In forgiveness, we are releasing energy that is incarcerating us in relation to someone else and in relation to our own self-inflicted wounds. However, learning of my propensity toward empathy (that invariably drained my own energy), I learned to consider that the giving away of my energy in sympathy or otherwise could find me terribly depleted. I needed to be mindful of that, measuring whether I felt energized or depleted in the company of others. In doing so, I became adept at realizing which people I no longer wanted to be around. There are so many lessons to be learned in each new spiritual practice. I began to practice forgiveness more readily.

It was easy enough for me to forgive Bob for all that had come to pass, for all the injustices he threw at me. He was leaving our world, and I would no longer need to deal with his intended abuses. Yet, I had learned to incorporate the lesson of forgiveness in relation to other relationships in my life, as well. The crux of forgiveness is that it is truly for the benefit of the one doing the forgiving.

If there were friends and family members who had chosen to turn their backs on me during this time of upheaval in our lives, I would learn that forgiving them for their lack of support didn't need to mean I had to reconcile a relationship with them. I could still forgive them their judgment or their disregard and choose to close the door on the once-upon-a-time relationship we once shared. I could vow to no longer allow myself to be treated with disregard, or disrespect, and understand that their judgment was theirs to carry, not mine. Making that decision and voicing that a new boundary was in place for me made forgiveness easy once again. Essentially, the more you practice forgiveness the easier it gets, and in it your heart remains open.

If you care to truly immerse yourself in this healing practice. you may want to explore the traditional Hawaiian practice of

Ho'oponopono, which is one of reconciliation and forgiveness often practiced by Indigenous South Pacific, Tahitian, and Samoan healers. Ho'oponopono is a call to peace and compassion — to fill the space that was once filled with discord with grace and forgiveness — so that forgiveness may spread its soothing balm overall. With no guilt or blame taken or assigned to another, it is a call to love, to let it rest without the need to talk about it so that we may come together at a later date in greater awareness and in love. You can find out more about the beautiful prayer and the practice of Ho'oponopono (which employs the use of the mantra, "I'm sorry, please forgive me, I love you, thank you.") with author and facilitator, Dr Joe Vitale.

Chapter 16

Old Shoes and Becoming Real

Sometimes the most unexpected things bring a renewal or a positive shift in your life that is bigger than you might have expected. I expected that changing places might do so, but not to the extent that it did. I moved from a big old house with many rooms and many closets to a little house with no closets (2500 square feet down to 900 square feet). I don't know why closets or lack thereof have significance, but they seem to in this case. No closets meant no more room for stacking stuff on shelves behind doors. In my new home there was only room for what was necessary and for keeping what was most treasured. In one simple move, I redefined what really mattered to me.

Now every picture hung and every corner filled held meaning for me; little things gifted from loved ones long gone and treasures from my past that still felt right because they reflected the real me adorned the rooms of my new humble abode. It felt as though

I had finally let go of an old pair of shoes I had been walking around in for the longest time. They were falling apart at the seams, yet they remained comfortable, so I didn't want to let them go. The top half was separating itself from the sole (like me from my soul). They were tattered and torn and no longer supportive (all so symbolically true of my life and the journey I had taken to heal it). But in making that journey from one house to another, I didn't take them with me. I threw them out. And I remembered all the things I had forgotten to do, and how to be me when I was wearing those old shoes.

Looking back on the journey I had forged, I wondered how many other times throughout my life had I come to a crossroads and made choices that I steadfastly *knew* left me no other choice to make? And I realized the answer was …never! Never before had there ever been only one right choice, even in not knowing precisely where it would lead. And I still don't know. But all of my tomorrows have become more present centered than ever. Living in the moment has never been so easy — trusting in the moment, in life, minute by minute, hour by hour, day by day. Trusting I will keep on breathing and trusting in my breath to bring me to the gentle emergence of peace has never been so easy. The absence of fear had brought me here. Winter has passed, and spring is here. I am here.

My healing heart journey did indeed heal the trauma of my past and set me on a path to greater fulfillment in life. But what happened inadvertently as I found my way home to myself was that I somehow just became more *real*. I am no longer afraid to let my vulnerabilities and my flaws show, to be myself even in the company of people whom I know simply won't get me. In authenticity, I can face my fears and my failures with courage and fortitude. In leaving my old self behind and all of my old stories finally dumped in the trash, I discovered a new self — one who has boundaries and respects other people's boundaries, one who knows now that my self-worth isn't connected to productivity and 'doing,' but simply in 'being' and in making new choices that support my self-care.

Now I am able to show up in the world, raw and ready, no apologies for being real, and eager to learn new lessons and continue to grow. *Whodathunk* I'd still be learning to grow up in my sixties! As I continue the journey to wholeness, I find myself craving the company of like-minded souls, of wanting to commune- in -unity (community), ready to expand my horizons, to be of service to others and to the world.

Connection with others is also essential to our well-being. We need to nurture quality relationships that invite us to lay our burdens down and witness one another's vulnerabilities and shortcomings and still feel safe. I find some old relationships falling away now, and new relationships wanting to be nurtured. I am finding my tribe. We witness and validate each other's suffering and successes. Sometimes when we're struggling to help ourselves, we can simply get out of our own way, and help someone else. We heal in common unity, as well.

My hope for this book is that it will introduce my readers to an open door of endless possibilities for healing oneself. That brings to mind a line that was narrated in one of my favorite movies, The Shawshank Redemption. When he was finally freed from his lifetime of incarceration the man expressed, "The world has gone and got itself in a big damn hurry." And so it is. But it's not going to change anytime soon. Time feels more accelerated than ever before. So, we may have to just slow down a little to make the time to nurture ourselves as we navigate that most honorable journey.

My roadmap and the themes therein are of self-exploration, of our wounds and our woe as the path to wisdom and wholeness, of surrender and trust, of taking responsibility, of forgiveness and gratitude, of prayer or sacred rituals practiced daily beyond the confines and narratives of religion, of the mind, body, and spirit connection. It is the ability to rewire our brains, the power of our thoughts to harm or to heal, of strengthening intuition and cultivating imagination, and of the awareness and insight to make changes. But above all else, the journey is about finding and holding the power of unconditional love (sacred and divine) to comfort and to heal. When you erase the restrictions you place on your love in fear that it will cost you something, you activate love's ability to empower yourself and others. And love paves the way every time, every step, on every journey.

The ancient Japanese art of 'Kintsukuroi' is to take something that is fatally flawed or broken and repair it with powdered gold, thereby transforming it to something beautiful. As we too may be fatally wounded or broken, so shall we heal and grow into a thing of beauty. The elements that help us to heal (love, forgiveness, prayer, etc.) are those that bind the wound into a scar of survival that is both beautiful and somehow sacred.

Walks in nature, meditations, dreamwork, kundalini, hatha, nigra, yin, or yoga in any form, Qigong, Falun Gong, Tai Chi, music and sound, drumming, dancing, humming, ritual, full moon and new moon circles, smudging.... There are so many ways to enhance your life with spiritual (or heart and soul centered) practices.

My heart is pure, my heart is gold. It leads me on as truths unfold. It shows me how, and why, and where, in gratitude with humble prayer.

You honestly don't have to spend thousands of dollars to get the help you need, to pursue the thing you want to do, to find joy and peace, happiness and contentment. Give to the world what it is you want to get, and all manner of good things will come your way.

There are guides and mentors everywhere, just waiting for you to ask or to recognize them as such. But your greatest ally is always 'you!' Follow your own sacred internal compass and trust in Spirit to guide you to where you want to get, and I promise you will *Love Your Life*.

Love your life with all its sham and drudgery, all its bumps and bruises, embracing the notion that life *doesn't happen to you, it happens through you*. All of it has been *created by you*, and *for you*, and it's up to you to make it right. And good.

Take responsibility, and nurture gratitude for all that you have, and all that will be, and for all the wonder in the world that you know to be true.

Generate a real and lasting relationship with your future self and the life you want to live by envisioning it repeatedly with eagerness and conviction. Break away from old patterns of self-defeating thoughts and behaviors that were self-sabotaging and dare to create the life you love. Act, speak and feel as if it is already true! The universe will pave the way of your choices and your desires.

Each and every one of us has the capacity not only to overcome suffering and uncertainty but to *overcome ourselves,* so that we may shift from our old self to a new self. It is a neurological, biological, conscientious shift. We have the capacity and the resources to recreate our circumstances and experience rebirth. We are all alchemists in our own lives with the power to transform our crisis (pain, heartbreak, depression, disease, etc.) into wisdom and growth.

We don't have to wait for the crisis to decide it's time for growth and change. The universe taps us on the shoulder to let us know that this might be the time. Unfortunately, more often than not, we just don't listen to those little taps on the shoulder and gentle nudges of discomfort, and when we don't listen, the universe may well decide to kick us in the teeth! I believe so many crises could be avoided if we'd simply listen the first time around. So, we might more often ask ourselves, "What lesson is trying to find me?" And listen carefully for the answer.

Happiness is not something we need to pursue, it is something we need to *uncover* within ourselves, and it's every person's birthright. Happy people believe in a benevolent universe, in a spirit that guides them as their soul connects to that universe, and they believe that life conspires for their well-being and for their good. Happy people show up in the world as victors, not victims. In *Peace, Love and Healing*, by Bernie Siegal M.D., he cites that there are a number of personality traits that identify a survivor, and the first is that survivorship behavior in itself eliminates the victim role and celebrates life. He adds that all survivors have a sense of meaning and purpose in their lives, they have the capacity to ask for help, and the capacity to view their diagnosis as an opportunity to direct their lives toward something better. Just as charcoal can become a diamond under pressure, so, too, can you become healed and whole under the pressure of illness or despair.

Survivors who learn to thrive incorporate laughter and humor into their daily lives and add playfulness and creativity to their regimes. One such immensely helpful activity is journal writing so that you never find yourself suffering in silence, even if you are only getting it out of your system with written words on paper. When our wounds are felt and validated, they can be worked on. Another essential component of spirituality is the practice of 'love.' Survivors choose to grow beyond their old stories. Our bodies are incarnate so that we may navigate our planet, and every cell in our body is capable of memory and consciousness, but we are all so much bigger than our bodies, for our souls are not finite, and are infinitely awakened into being receptive to the sacred and the divine, through our hearts.

Remember the old game Truth or Dare? I challenge you to find your truth and dare you to live it through your heart. The first organ to form in the human body is the heart. It, too, is divine. Now, as I move forward, and follow my heart every step of the way, *I love my life!*

Epilogue

Sometimes out of the blue an old trauma will resurface and send you spinning, and you wonder why. My manuscript was complete, and I had submitted it for publication, and I felt good about having shared little pearls of wisdom I had gathered along the way of my healing journey, when out of the blue, many years later, an old nightmare came raging in.

This one arrived in the shadow of a new moon, when the darkness was thick and deep.

His ghost came toward me as I lay in bed in the pitch black of the night. I was frozen in fear as he lay beside me and gripped my arm so I couldn't move. I was somehow aware I was dreaming, though that didn't make it any less real. I called in the light to give me strength, telling myself he was no longer a man of flesh and bone, yet I struggled to free myself from his threatening grip, and lashed out with my words.

"Go! Leave!"

I tried biting his arm, but my teeth met only air, so I struggled to awaken in prayer.

Upon awakening, I pressed my palms together firmly at my heart, and waited till the racing of my heart abated. I whispered to myself, "I am alone, and I am safe in my bed."

As always, I have an urge to pee, and it comes every five minutes for the next hour or more; flushing, flushing. I flick on my bedside lamp and pick up my novel as I long for distraction to other worlds where ghosts don't roam. But my journal calls out to me. I'm eager to find out what my soul has to say to me.

I don't understand why he still comes back to haunt me. He had been gone for so long. But I don't have to understand. I just have to remember that ghosts always tread in the darkness, and they can't hurt me if I'm standing in the light.

It is spring, and I know that the days will grow longer now. The new moon will grow full again and the days will grow longer, the light will linger through long summer days. The summer sun will seep deep into my bones and give me strength and resilience and energy to burn, like the fire that resides in the heart of the summer sun. I feel warm, and safe. I no longer have to survive. I thrive. The nightmare has faded. Bladder empty, heart at peace.

My pulse beats a steady rhythm as I walk upon the earth. I consider that I am as insignificant as a grain of sand, and as significant as God in all her power and glory. Seasons turn and tides shift. Organs and joints and tendons and ligaments bend and stretch, and blood pumps through my veins while mother earth breathes beneath my feet.

What an adventure to have been given a body to travel here, with a mind as infinite as a galaxy of star seeds, a heart as powerful as medicine and magic, and a soul omnipotent as eternity. Despite it all, bad dreams and demons, and the human condition which grants us discomfort for the evolution of our souls, how can I not love my life? I am here. I am standing in the light.

Ingram Content Group UK Ltd.
Milton Keynes UK
UKHW010829180723
425342UK00001B/50

9 798765 242995